The Rise of the Right in BENGAL

The Rise of the Right in BENGAL

Animesh Biswas

PRABHAT PAPERBACKS

Published by
PRABHAT PAPERBACKS
4/19 Asaf Ali Road,
New Delhi-110 002 (INDIA)
e-mail: prabhatbooks@gmail.com

ISBN 978-93-90378-38-8
The Rise of the Right in BENGAL
by Shri Animesh Biswas

Edition
First, 2021

Price
₹ 200.00 (Rupees Two Hundred only)

Printed at
R-Tech Offset Printers, Delhi

Foreword

The Bengal, at present time popularly known as 'Pashchim Banga' or 'Pashchim Bangal' or 'West Bengal' undoubtedly was the epicentre of the Nationalist movement inspired by a monk who wore saffron as his identity and a glorious mind of Bengal, popularly known as Swami Vivekananda. His perspective of a Hindu-Rashtra provided a basis for questioning colonialism and inspired the independence movements against the British Raj. Swami Vivekananda (Narendra Nath Dutta) strongly sculpted the idea of awakening 'Bharat Mata' and after 118 years of his demise, another 'Narendra' (Prime Minister Narendra Modi) echoed the same melodious chant 'Bharat Mata ki Jai', in his first election rally for 2019 West Bengal Lok Sabha election speech at Coochbehar.

'The rise of Right in Bengal' is a book based upon the truth hidden beneath a huge leftist narrative which is a biased and prejudiced version of a partial truth where Ramakrishna Paramhansa was vividly portrayed as a Kali devotee but not as one of the main contributors of Bengal renaissance and the source of a brilliant idea—Ramakrishna order. Leftist narrative of course portrayed Swami Vivekananda as a great monk but never discussed much of him as the key person of Hindu revivalism and his idea of Hindu–Rashtra, which had a huge impact on the Indian independence movement.

I believe, this book should provide a good insight into the history of Bengal (Now West Bengal) and how Dharma is the soul of all of us. The writer has also given an account of the Bhakti Movement of Shri Chaitanya Dev and Shri Ramakrishna Paramhanshna, a follower of Bhakti tradition and introduced Ramakrishna order, the spirit of Sangha which highly influenced Swami Vivekananda. Swamiji in Chicago makes the world understand the idea of our great knowledge, Hinduism, and Nationalism (राष्ट्रीयता). Nationalism which comes from our Vedas is much different from western philosophy. Our Nationalism teaches us as the World is one family or Vasudhaiva Kutumbakam (वसुधैव कुटुम्बकम्)

Swami Vivekananda's nationalism was based on Dharma which is the Praan (प्राण) of everyone living here (the people of this land). Our Dharma is 'Sarv Samaveshak' (सर्वसमावेशक) which means 'All-inclusive'. Dharma is the duty and life's goal to have the same love/adore to all irrespective of gender, social and economical status.

The writer has also written about Swami Vivekananda to give a clear picture of Swamiji's deeper mind and perhaps the origin of his idea of Hindu-Rashtra, as Swamiji Said: "We are Hindus. In the core of our lives, we have the great teachings from Vedas and which are still practiced by us. The word Hindu doesn't only stand to represent our faith but also is a way of life that cuts across many religious beliefs and stands for everything glorious."

Swami Vivekananda's message to the Hindus was to get out of their hypnotised state of mind, awaken their 'sleeping soul' and propagate the message of peace and blessings given by the 'ancient Mother' to the world. Like Vivekananda, Aurbindo Ghosh and Mahatma Gandhi also realised that Dharma and spirituality are in the veins of Indians and worked for India's unification through awakening the force of Dharma and spirituality. And to understand these discourses, anybody interested in Bengal and Indian Nationalism should read this book which may lead to a further course of debate and discussion.

In the words of Parampujya Sarsanghchalakji Dr. Mohan Bhagwat, our Dharma goes beyond just tolerance (सहिष्णुता), it is also about believing on contradicting views not just accepting the opinion itself. He says the system should be equitable and exploitative. Until everyone gets happiness, eternal happiness is a day dream (व्यवस्था समता युक्त और शोषण-मुक्त होनी चाहिए। जब तक सभी को सुख प्राप्त नहीं होता, तब तक शाश्वत सुख दिवास्वप्न है।)

'The Rise of Right in Bengal' written by Animesh Biswas is an investigation of why the Marichjhapi incident, a case of violence against Bengali Hindus in independent India, happened in the communist regime of Bengal? The book raises the question of whether communist and socialist ideology failed to understand the crisis of Hindu refugees from East Pakistan (now Bangladesh).

This book may give us strong indulgence to a deep dive into the vast area of forgotten history and historians from Bengal. It may be disturbing but pertinent questions that this book has raised on the policy of communist party of India in 1947 and how an unfair piece of history distorted the role of Syama Prasad Mookerjee's strong opposition against the Muslim League's demand to include the undivided (East and West) Bengal in Pakistan though he was highly supported by the Bengali Hindus and stalwarts like Dr. Bidhan Chandra Roy, R.C. Majumder, Sir Jadunath Sarkar, and others from the Western part of Bengal. Today's Pashchim Banga (West Bengal) would not have been a part of the Indian Republic if Syama Prasad would not have stood like a true son of 'Bharat

Mata' against the Muslim League and also against a sinister plot for a United Bengal by the then prime minister of Bengal province, Huseyn Shaheed Suhrawardy. All these historical details have been carefully mentioned in this book.

One of the most interesting parts of this book reveal the roadmap of 'Right' narrative in West Bengal (2014–2019 mainly), under the leadership of Amit Shah and crafted with details on how Bharatiya Janata Party becomes popular in West Bengal. The book vividly describes the influence of Amit Shah's Mission Bengal 2019 and ended with a strong line as the author writes—'Bengal was waiting for a Hindu Aura of Authority'—Narendra Modi .

Bengal has been ahead during the struggle of freedom, it has been the birthplace of Ramkrishna Paramhans and Swami Vivekananda. My life has been inspired by Swamiji's teaching to a great extent. Aurobindo's greatness needs no introduction but it's a duty of each generation to share the lives of the greats to the next one. For decades West Bengal has been disconnected from the development path the country has been marching upon. Bengal or West Bengal needs to connect back to its roots of Nationalism, with a rich history of Nationalist way of life Bengal is getting back to its core.

Mahatma Gandhi said, 'Hinduism is a relentless pursuit after truth and if today it has become dormant, inactive, irresponsive to growth, it is because we are fatigued, and as soon as the fatigue is over, Hinduism will burst forth upon the world with a brilliance perhaps unknown before.'

That's why Hindu Dharma is a loving and tolerant Dharma. The coming generations need to know about their duties towards their Dharma which has kept on enlightening the world for thousands of years.

We are fortunate that we are born as child of Bharat

Mata. Bharat Rashtra has been much before any civilisation took shape. In Atharva Veda the birth of this nation is clearly mentioned.

भद्रमिच्छन्तः ऋषयः स्वर्विदस्तपोदीक्षामुपनिषेदुरग्रे।
ततोराष्टंऊबलमोजश्च जातंतदस्मैंदेवा उपसंनमन्तु।।

अथर्ववेद
(19.41)

The mantra is telling us that in order to strengthen the spirit of the nation, our sages moulded their lives into austerity and initiation, and then the power and strength of the nation was born. Here, tenacity means to follow the duty, and initiation means teaching self-righteousness. Both things are very important. Tenacity and initiation take place in the life of a teacher, from them he builds his students, and by being influenced by these qualities of that teacher, students become child of Nation. This is same vision of our Dharma which enables every soul (Atma) living on this great Rashtra and has a divine duty towards the well-being of every creature by accomplishing his Karma.

It should be a common goal of every Bharatiya to work towards restoring the glory of West Bengal which has given us so many great personalities—Bankim Chandra, Ramakrishna Paramhans, Swami Vivekananda, Shri Aurobindo, Rabindranath Tagore, Netaji Subhas Chandra Bose, Dr. Syama Prasad Mukherjee and many more. To achieve this we need to know about the past and the coming generations should be told about the correct description of the past.

I wish the writer a success. I am sure that readers will gain knowledge from this book.

—Shiv Prakash
National Joint General Secretary
(Organisation)
Bharatiya Janata Party

Editor's Note

On 16th August 1946 the ruling party of Undivided Bengal, the Muslim League, began its Direct Action against the Hindus. Kolkata turned red from the bloodshed of thousands of helpless Hindus. At least 10,000 people lost their lives and 100,000 residents were left homeless in Calcutta within 72 hours. The next day Bengal media reported Suhrawardy Government and the Muslim League for the deadly violence.

After 73 years in 2019, the Bharatiya Janata Party secured 18 seats from West Bengal in the 2019 Lok Sabha Elections, a gain of 800 percentage from its 2014 tally proved that Bengal was waiting for a Hindu Aura of Authority and that is Narendra Modi, the most powerful leader of Bharat after much regarded mass leader Syama Prasad Mookerjee from Bengal.

It is important to understand that the BJP could never have gained ground in Bengal if they did not speak of issues that hold great significance for Hindus of Syama Prasad's Bengal and the misgovernance of Mamata Banerjee. Illegal immigration, minority appeasement, communal violence– all these issues are of significant importance to the Bengal electorate. The BJP rose to prominence in the state riding on the promise to address them. The major fact was that the Hindu voters of the Left crossed over to the BJP in the 2019 Lok Sabha elections and this crossover has largely been motivated by concerns that revolve around their Hindu identity. And not just Hindu upper castes, but also Other Backward Classes, Scheduled Castes and Scheduled Tribes voted for the BJP in large proportions. Some said, Rise of Right wing in Bengal started in Ram Navami 2017 but it started actually in 2011 when Mamata Banerjee came in power with a strong support of RSS and Atal Bihari Vajpayee of Bharatiya Janata Party.

Bengal—the heartland of Nationalism portrayed by Swami Vivekananda, Anandamath and Syama Prasad Mookerjee—embraced a perfect ecology for the growth of Right wing ideology based on 'Joto Mot Toto Poth' by Ramakrishna Paramhansa which has been echoed in Narendra Modi 's voice when he said, "Sab ki Sath, Sab ki Bikash, Sab ka Vishwas."

I started my journey through journalism 30 years ago, migrated from Asansol to Kolkata. I had seen many socio-political changes in this land of Nationalism, met many big leaders of different political parties and listened their own political philosophy or agenda but never witnessed any vibration which made Syama Prasad Mookerjee a mass leader in Bengal, the land of Hindu Homeland movement.

On the eve of 2019 Lok Sabha election, my long time friend and a humble SwayamSevak Animesh Biswas invited me in his project 'Rise of Right in West Bengal' and asked my opinion. My instant reaction was, "Which Bengal you are talking about my beloved brother; let me first know about that. There are many shades of history of Bengal and that's why it may be confusing but very easy to understand this land of our nationalist identity." Animesh Biswas smiled and said "No doubts that I love to discover Bengal through the piece of history emerged from the mind of Sir Jadunath Sarkar, Ramesh Chandra Mazumder and Rakhal Das Bandopadhyay and that is the body and mind in this land of tolerance and confluence then the spirit must be Ramakrishna Sangha, Swami Vivekananda and VandeMataram."

I am delighted that Bengal is going to embrace, not an emotional fiction but the sharpest reportage without any theoretical baggage from Animesh Biswas. This book is his first expression of a vast project called 'Rise of Right in Bengal'.

It has been a pleasurable journey to edit the book and a matter of happiness to see a young mind bringing his work to the world.

Wish him best of luck.

—Jayanta Guha

Acknowledgment

Writing this book has been an immense learning experience for me. Coming from West Bengal and bottom in North India it was a journey of self-learning rather than just putting my experience to paper.

As a swayamsevak, my learning has been around the greats of Swami Vivekananda, Ramakrishna Paramhansa, Shri Aurobindo, and many more icons live as it is the core of our add ideology. I have been engaged with Bharatiya Janata Party's hard work and have seen the sacrifices made by co-workers in West Bengal.

As a student of politics, it has been an extraordinary experience for the contemporary social, economic, and political situation in Bengal. While working in the 2019 Lok Sabha elections in West Bengal, I had an opportunity to travel across West Bengal and I could see the change Bengal is waiting for. The Lok Sabha results in 2019 proved that the country decisively chose Narendra Modi as it's a true leader by leaps and bounds.

While I came across many intellectuals, journalists, political scientists and politicians who themselves never anticipated the result. No exit poll except only one gave considerable chance to BJP in West Bengal for the thumping win which they got in 2019.

BJP won 18 seats whereas Trinamool Congress got 22 seats and BJP's vote rose to 41%–just 3.5% short Trinamool Congress's share. Interestingly BJP was not able to win any seat in the last phase which was due to a lower percentage of votes' turnout due to the TMC sponsored violence in Kolkata. If you study other phases, BJP was much ahead of Trinamool Congress.

क्रियासिद्धिः सत्त्वेभवति महतां नोपकरणे ॥

kriyasiddhi satvebhavati mahatma nopakarane

Meaning—

The actions of great people are accomplished by their inner strength, not by the means (resources) of doing it.

This was said by Parampujya Sarsanghchalak Dr. Mohan Bhagwatji during one of his speech in Kolkata in 2017. He rightly said that means are not important; it is the inner strength which takes you to the goal.

It is an important result that has been discussed in the book further. I am too junior to express my gratitude and thankfulness to Man. Shiv Prakashji who inspires thousands of BJP workers like me. He is of firm belief that nationalism can rise again in the land of Shri Aurobindo and Bankimchandra. In an election meeting in Kolkata where he said, "We are here not to win but to kindle a new positive change which is led by Shri Narendra Modi . The change will enable violence-free, fearless living, and upliftment of Democratic rights. What we do today will define our future." This inspired me to collect my views and observations in West Bengal. Its a dream come true when he agreed to my request of writing the Introduction of the book.

I'm also thankful to Editor Shri Jayanta Guha to enable the collection of my thoughts and views. This book would not have been possible if my life partner Dr. Rinku Biswas would not have encouraged me to write and give constant support and sparing me for writing . My son Atharv's childish positivity have also kept me energised. As a child, I will always be proud to hand over a copy to my parents, who are the force and inspiration for me.

This book would not have been possible without so many friends and contributors; names of all of them cannot be mentioned here but I sincerely express my gratitude towards them.

The facts and descriptions in the book are my own and I have tried to collate my research and observation in the best possible way. The narration and description of the book are based upon my primary and secondary research, with great help from my editor. After the state assembly election results of for the coming in West Bengal I'll be adding a final chapter of the book because Nationalism (Rashtriyata) is in the heart of West Bengal and it is time that the vision of greats like Swami Vivekanada, Shri Aurobindo, Bankim Chandra, Netaji Subhash Chamdra Bose, Dr. Syama Prasad Mookerjee and many more should be realised now.

I humbly dedicated my work to Rashtriya Swyamsevak Sangh and thank all the Pracharak's who have relentlessly worked on Vyakti Nirman (Character building for Nation). I have been fortunate to be come from the great family of Swyamsevaks which have the likes of great Shri Deendayal Upadhaya, Shri Atal Bihari Vajpayee, Shri Lal Krishna Advani, Shri Amit Shah, Shri Jagat Prakash Nadda and our Honorable Prime Minister Shri Narendra Modi.

—Animesh Biswas

Contents

Contents

Renaissance of Hindu religion and the concept of *Hindu Rashtra* in Bengal

"Any country would have been proud to have a personality like Vivekananda. But the Marxists and Left progressives in Bengal are a different breed. They are now threatened to be buried in the quicksand of their frothy Marxist ideology that is completely unrelated to the psyche of Bengal..." (Organiser, the RSS organ) which is realized by the many left intellectuals, much before BJP bagged 18 Lok Sabha seats in 'Left and Secular' Bengal in 2019.

After the death of Syama Prasad Mookerjee in 1953, the left and center-left block of Indian politics tried to restructure the social-psyche by importing foreign ideologies and perceptions, but their alien ideology and bad governance made them irrelevant in Bengal. The minority appeasement and politics of intolerance might have been a compulsion for CPI(M) and Mamata Banerjee's vote bank politics but that wasn't the soul of Bengal. Many years ago, the Bhakti movement in Bengal led by Shri Chaitanyadev showed the concept of inclusive culture to whole India, which is at present the mantra of a visionary man-once a humble RSS Pracharak and now the Prime Minister of India—Narendra Modi and his future vision of 'New India'.

Bengal–the land of Bhakti Yoga

Shri Chaitanyadev-the champion of the Bhakti (devotion) movement, denounced the caste system and stood for universal brotherhood. He lived for only forty-seven years (1486–1533) but the inspiration of his Bhakti yoga is still very much relevant in the Bengali Hindu mind in Bengal. Chaitanyadev and his philosophy of Bhakti Yoga shook the very foundation of Indian society. Bhakti movement did not fight with arms, but with musical instruments; the goal was not to conquer other countries but to conquer the hearts of people. His "mantra" was not "to hate", but "to love". Chaitanyadev introduced Kirtan or devotional recitation and singing of religious songs in processions through villages and cities. This public recitation and singing were a powerful publicity weapon and these city-processions were meant to demonstrate organisational power. When the Kazi or the Bengal ruler banned Kirtan, Shri Chaitanyadev challenged the illegal threat of Kazi and like a dauntless lion, he organized a rally of common men and compelled Kazi to withdraw his order. It was for the first time in the history of India, people will win over the state power under the leadership of a devotional movement led by Shri Chaitanyadev.

> ***Chaitanyadev and his philosophy of Bhakti Yoga shook the very foundation of Indian society. Bhakti movement did not fight with arms, but with musical instruments; the goal was not to conquer other countries but to conquer the hearts of people.***

The philosophies of the Bhakti movement originated even before Chaitanyadev, essentially through the Vaisnava lyrics written by the pre-Chaitanya poets, mainly Chandidas (14th century) and Vidyapati (1380–1460) but Chaitanyadev added a new dimension to the movement, and it was through his leadership that it developed into a social movement. He adopted the concept of jivatma (the human soul) and paramatma (eternal soul) and added to it the idea of Dvaita-Advaita tattva, the idea of the simultaneous diversity and unity of God and soul.

There were two compulsions for Chaitanyadev to start his movement: one, to reform his religion and society and, second, to counteract the ever-increasing influence of Islam. During this period, society was severely constricted by the caste system and social discrimination and by such practices as Satidaha, kulinism, child marriage, ex-communication, penance, etc. Shri Chaitanyadev fought against the social abuses and also gave the common people equal rights in his religion of love. He endeavoured to create a Hindu society in which people of all castes would follow the same religious rites and thus come closer to each other. This was the strength of the Hindu Vaisnava movement or Bhakti movement. Shri Chaitanyadev raised new movement against conservatism, superstition and opened its portals to the common man, irrespective of caste, creed, religion, gender, and nationality. Bhakti movement embraced the untouchable, honoured the womenfolk, and protected the weak and the vulnerable.

Shri Chaitanyadev raised new movement against conservatism, superstition and opened its portals to the common man, irrespective of caste, creed, religion, gender, and nationality.

The path of Bhakti Yoga pulled everybody's attention as a devotional tool to protest and reform the pride and prejudice of a system. But in Bengal, there is strong evidence of Shakti

Yoga too, whose powerful but unarmed resistance threatened the pride of British Raj for 50 long years. In Bengal, this mighty revolt, popularly known as Sanyasi Revolt (1770–1820), was the inspiration of Bande Mataram poem written by Bankim Chandra Chatterjee in his 1882 novel 'Anandamath'.

Shakti Yoga: Inspiration of Bande Mataram

Soon after the Battle of Plassey and Buxar, the British gradually established their political and economic hegemony over large parts of India. This resulted in changes in the economic, social, religious, and political spheres of life, as many people getting stripped off their traditional rights and privileges and faced the high tide of poverty, which led to the famine of 1770. These were the reasons for many uprisings against the British. The most notable Politico–Religious movement among those uprisings was the Sannyasi-Fakir movement (1770–1820).

After the British had acquired revenue rights in Bengal, many zamindars had fallen upon hard times owing to the steep tax rates. It was the practice of the Sannyasis to collect alms and contributions from these zamindars during their religious travels. This was stopped when the zamindars found it too difficult to provide alms since after paying the British their dues, they were hardly left with anything substantial. The Sannyasis who had protested against the English in the 18th century were many sects of Sannyasis, who travelled from Northern India to various religious places and shrines in Bengal. These Sannyasis were mostly Vedic yogis belonging to the Giri and Puri groups of 'Ek Dandi sannyasis'. The British were wary of these wandering men and called them by various epithets like 'erratic beggars', 'gypsies of Hindusthan', 'lawless mendicants', 'religious vagrants', etc. The British considered the

Sannyasis looters and imposed restrictions on the Sannyasis, barring them from visiting holy places. The Sannyasis rose in protest against the British and raided English factories and government treasuries. The rebellion was centered in the forests of Murshidabad and Baikunthapur, Jalpaiguri, Bengal. In 1771, 150 unarmed Fakirs traveling in Bengal were killed under the orders of Warren Hastings. These Fakirs were mostly from the Madarika sect.

In the Sannyasi Fakir Revolt, the Fakirs and Sannyasis came together for the rebellion to defeat their common enemy- the British. The rebels mainly engaged in guerilla warfare. They knew the countryside better than the British army and they could disappear at a moment's notice. This was their main secret of survival against the military giant-the British army. The Sannyasi uprising went on for about 50 years and was suppressed completely only in the 1820s.

Bankim Chandra Chatterjee's 1882 novel Anandamath was set in the backdrop of the Sannyasi Rebellion. Bankim Chandra introduced Bande Mataram poem in his novel and Bande Mataram became a powerful mantra of the whole nation for independence from British rule.

Bankim Chandra Chatterjee's 1882 novel Anandamath was set in the backdrop of the Sannyasi Rebellion. Bankim Chandra introduced Bande Mataram poem in his novel and Bande Mataram became a powerful mantra of the whole nation for independence from British rule. But then, Bengal was looking for a great event, a revival of Hindu religion, which was initiated by Chaitanyadev

Influence of Ramakrishna Order and the emergence of Nationalism in Bengal

"Atmano moksharthang jagaddhitaya cha"–liberation from the bondage of misery-go-round of life in the limitless joy of the Infinite after attainment of what nothing else remains to be attained, and the way is self-expansion or loving all as extended self, identifying with the ultimate solidarity of one life, expressed as many–this was the main Mantra of Ramakrishna order or Sangha.

The two main objectives of the Sangha were to bring into existence a band of monks dedicated to a life of renunciation and practical spirituality and among them, teachers and workers would be sent out to spread the universal message of Vedanta as illustrated in the life of Ramakrishna...

The teachings of Ramakrishna Paramahansa (1836–86), one of the most prominent religious figures of India during the nineteenth century formed the basis of the Ramakrishna Sangha. The two main objectives of the Sangha were to bring into existence a band of monks dedicated to a life of renunciation and practical spirituality and among them, teachers and workers would be sent out to spread the universal message of Vedanta as illustrated in the life of Ramakrishna and in conjunction with other disciples to carry on preaching, philanthropic and charitable works, looking upon all men, women, and children, irrespective of caste, creed or colour, as veritable manifestations of the Divine.

Ramakrishna was a key figure in the revival of Hinduism in Bengal at a time, when the intense spiritual crisis was gripping the province, leading to the predominance of young Bengalis embracing Brahmoism and Christianity. His legacy did not end with his death in 1886; his most prominent disciple, Swami Vivekananda carried on his teachings and philosophy to the world through Ramakrishna Mission.

If Ramakrishna was the spiritual founder of the Ramakrishna Movement, Vivekananda stands out as the movement's chief organizer and publicist. His speech at Chicago in 1893 established him as the greatest figure in the Parliament of World Religions and India as the Mother of religion. Greeting the youngest of the nations on behalf of "the most ancient order of monks in the world, the Vedic order of sannyasins, a religion which has taught the world both tolerance and universal acceptance".

Swami Vivekananda at the world Parliament of Religions, Chicago, 1893

Swami Vivekananda's nationalism is associated with spiritualism and love for motherland. He linked India's regeneration to her age-old tradition of the spiritual goal. His nationalism is based on Humanism and Universalism, the two cardinal features of Indian spiritual culture. The nature of his nationalism is not materialistic but purely spiritual, which is considered to be the source of all strength of Indian life. Unlike western nationalism, which is secular, Swami Vivekananda's nationalism was based on religion which is the lifeblood of the Indian people. Like Vivekananda, Aurobindo Ghosh, and Mahatma Gandhi also realized that religion and spirituality are in the veins of Indians and worked for India's unification through awakening the force of religion and spirituality.

Swami Vivekananda's vision of a *Hindu Rashtra*

In the nineteenth century, the era of 'Modern Hinduism', cradled many Hindu revivalist thoughts and reform movements. These led to the fresh interpretations of the ancient scriptures of Upanishads and Vedanta and also emphasized on social reform, and we can attain this thought-provoking idea from the words and work of a young Indian Hindu monk of the nineteenth century–Swami Vivekananda. On the context of 'Hindu', his self-esteem was always high as the Himalayas:

We are Hindus. I do not use the word Hindu in any bad sense at all, nor do I agree with those that think there is any bad meaning in it. In old times, it simply meant people who lived on the other side of the Indus; today, a good many among those who hate us may have put a bad interpretation upon it, but names are nothing. Upon us depends whether the name Hindu will stand for everything that is glorious, everything that is spiritual, or whether it will remain a name of opprobrium, one designating the downtrodden, the worthless, the heathen. If at present, the word Hindu means anything bad, never mind; by our action, let us be ready to show that this is the highest word that any language can invent.

Swami Vivekananda's message to the Hindus was to get

out of their hypnotized state of mind, awaken their "sleeping soul" and propagate the message of peace and blessings given by the "ancient Mother" to the world. Vivekananda was so deeply influenced by the powerful sloka of Katha Upanishad that he used that several times in his lectures. On 12 November 1896, he said when delivering a speech at Lahore:

Therefore, young men of Lahore, raise once more that mighty banner of Advaita, for on no other ground can you have that wonderful love until you see that the same Lord is present everywhere. Unfurl that banner of love! "Arise, awake, and stop not till the goal is reached." Arise, arise once more, for nothing can be done without renunciation.

Swami Vivekananda's mission was to reconstruct and regenerate the nation. To him, the national regeneration depended upon two things-revitalization and renovation of India's religion, "the central theme of her national life" and the remoulding of Indian society. The first thing which he said to his compatriots was not to imitate the West. To him, the moment India tried to become Europe, she was destined to die. Indian society or religion was not to be reformed on Western lines. What was required was a reinterpretation of religion in a manner acceptable to the modern mind and the readjustment of social structure which would establish social mobility.

Swami Vivekananda's mission was to reconstruct and regenerate the nation. To him, the national regeneration depended upon two things-revitalization and renovation of India's religion, "the central theme of her national life" and the remoulding of Indian society.

Vivekananda re-interpreted Advaita Vedanta, presenting it as the essence of Hindu spirituality, and the development of human religiosity. This reinterpretation produced neo-Vedanta, in which Advaita Vedanta was combined with disciplines, such as yoga and the concept of social service to attain perfection from the ascetic traditions in what Vivekananda called the "practical Vedanta". The practical side essentially included participation in social reform.

He also asked the Indians to look to India's ancient traditions, which were rooted in the Vedas and Upanishads, which preached the universal unity and to draw inspiration from them; He was the first to tell his countrymen that every nation has what might be described as a national elan and national destiny. To some it may be politics, to some, it may be religion. Indians were destined to garner all the spiritual values to combine them and to concentrate them, to preserve them so that at a suitable moment of need, India may flood the world. His method was to preserve the past by reconstructing it and thus, he preached a philosophy of "preservation by reconstruction. "

> ***This universalism and humanism of Swamiji make his philosophy modern. This particular aspect attracted both the Moderates and Right political spectrum of Indian freedom struggle to his philosophy.***

But at the same time, he preached a philosophy of synthesis-a synthesis between the East and the West. He was the one who found in the British connection, a potent means for breaking the moribund Indian society and civilization of his time. In his personality was shed the past and the present, ancient wisdom and modern knowledge. He was a Hindu to the backbone, but he loved other religions as well. His was not the role of a reactionary patriot, who would take his country away from the assimilation of other cultures. He loved India, but he loved humanity too, particularly the poor and the downtrodden masses. This universalism and humanism of Swamiji make his philosophy modern. This particular aspect attracted both the Moderates and Right political spectrum of Indian freedom struggle to his philosophy.

Impact of Swami Vivekananda's message on Nationalist Movement of India

It was so obvious to fall in love with the idea of Hindu Nation of Swami Vivekananda, for any Hindu and a nationalist leader like Mahatma Gandhi or Shri Aurobindo or Bal Gangadhar Tilak or Bipin Chandra Pal.

Vivekananda's nationalist thoughts deified the nation and seeded the freedom movement. The British Police repeatedly found Swami's literature in the hands of the freedom fighters and revolutionaries, even mulled action against the Ramakrishna Math.

When Bipin Chandra Pal felt, Vivekananda's message was "the message of modern humanity", then Bal Gangadhar Tilak's observation was:

"Twelve centuries ago, Sankaracharya was the only great personality, who not only spoke of the purity of our religion, not only uttered in words that this religion was our strength and wealth, not only said that it was our sacred duty to preach this religion in the length and breadth of the world–but also brought all this into action. Swami Vivekananda is a person of that stature—who appeared towards the last half of the 19th century."

Vivekananda's nationalist thoughts deified the nation and seeded the freedom movement. The British Police repeatedly found Swami's literature in the hands of the freedom fighters and revolutionaries, even mulled action against the Ramakrishna Math.

Swamiji's vision of the Hindu Nation also became a main inspiration for the nationalist viewpoint in today's India. One of the most respected leaders of the Rashtriya Swayamsevak Sangh (RSS), Balasaheb Apte's lifelong pet sentence was "Vivekananda is like Gita for the RSS." Swami Vivekananda's Rousing Call to the Hindu Nation published in 1963, edited by the leader of Rashtriya Swayamsevak Sangh, Eknath Ranade,- where we can witness that in his eloquent speech Swamiji shaping the indestructible narrative of Hindu Rashtra or Hindu Nation :

Swami Vivekananda in during his visit to England

O ye Hindus, de-hypnotise yourselves

Let us proclaim to every soul: Arise, awake, and stop not till the goal is reached. Arise, awake! Awake from this hypnotism of weakness. None is really weak; the soul is infinite, omnipotent, and omniscient. Stand up, assert yourself, proclaim the God within you, do not deny Him! Too much of inactivity, too much of weakness, too much of hypnotism has been and is upon our race. O ye modern Hindus, de-hypnotise yourselves. The way to do that is found in your own sacred books. Teach yourselves, teach everyone his real nature, call upon the sleeping soul and see how it awakes. Power will come, glory will come, goodness will come, purity will come, and everything that is excellent will come when this sleeping soul is roused to self-conscious activity.

Rejuvenated Glorious Bharat

I do not see into the future; nor do I care to see. But one vision I see dear as life before me: that the ancient Mother has awakened once more, sitting on Her throne rejuvenated, more glorious than ever. Proclaim Her to all the world with the voice of peace and benediction.

□

Confluence of different shapes of Nationalism in Indian Independence Movement

Hindu Cultural Nationalism (सांस्कृतिक राष्ट्रवाद) and Indian Nationalism are same

The partition of Bengal (1905) triggered the Hindus of Bengal. The Bengali Hindus began an angry agitation, as younger members started agitations against the British power. Nationalists all over India supported the Bengali cause and were shocked at the British disregard for opinion and ostensible divide and rule strategy. The protest spread to Bombay, Poona, and Punjab. Lord Curzon had believed that the Congress was no longer an effective force but provided it with a cause to rally the public around and gain fresh strength from.

The partition also caused embarrassment to the Indian National Congress. A division opened in the Indian National Congress between the moderates led by Gopal Krishna Gokhale, who downplayed public agitation, and the narrative of Hindu cultural nationalism led by the nationalist leader Bal Gangadhar Tilak, who tried to mobilise Indians by appealing to an explicitly Hindu political identity using the press and by evoking occasions like Ganesh Chaturthi and our faith for cow to create unrest against the British administration in India.

Under the influence of such leaders, the political discourse of the Congress moved from polite accusation against the imperial rule to the stronger claim of Tilak that "Swaraj is my birthright and I will have it".

Bal-Lal-Pal

Tilak opposed the moderate views of Gopal Krishna Gokhale and was supported by fellow Indian nationalists Lala Lajpat Rai in Punjab and Bipin Chandra Pal in Bengal, known as the Modern Hindu Reformer of India. He had no faith in mild protests in the form of non-cooperation with the British colonialists. Shri Aurobindo referred to him as one of the mightiest prophets of nationalism.

Bipin Chandra Pal had founded the nationalist Bengali newspaper Bande Mataram in 1906. Pal invited Aurobindo to become its editor along with Pal. The paper rapidly became a major success and the nationalist views finally found a popular voice.

To take the view of Hindu

Cultural Nationalism to the public, Bipin Chandra Pal had founded the nationalist Bengali newspaper Bande Mataram in 1906. Pal invited Aurobindo to become its editor along with Pal. The paper rapidly became a major success and the nationalist views finally found a popular voice. But as a result of its popularity and open espousal of aggressive methods, the paper came into frequent confrontation with the Raj.

In 1907, the annual session of the Congress Party was held at Surat, Gujarat. Trouble broke out over the selection of the new president of the Congress between the moderate and the reformist sections of the party. The party split led by Tilak-Pal-Lajpat Rai ("Lal-Bal-Pal triumvirate") and the moderate faction. Nationalists like Aurobindo Ghosh, V.O. Chidambaram Pillai supported Bal Gangadhar Tilak.

In the same year in 1907, the British Government decided to prosecute the group behind Bande Mataram, for its constant agitation against British rule. Notices were served for using language which was a "direct incentive to violence and lawlessness." On August 16, Aurobindo was sought for arrest by the Police. Aurobindo courted arrest and was released on monetary sureties. The sensational act and the events surrounding the arrest were seen as an episode of defiance against the empire and turned him into a national celebrity. Provincial and National press showered lavish praise on Aurobindo and Rabindranath Tagore wrote:

"Rabindranath, O Aurobindo, bows to thee! O friend, my country's friend, O Voice incarnate, free, Of India's soul.... The fiery messenger that with the lamp of God hath come...Rabindranath, O Aurobindo, bows to thee".

The prosecution was unable to establish that Shri Aurobindo was the editor of the paper and he was acquitted. Bipin Chandra Pal was sentenced to six months in prison for declining to depose. After the Bande Mataram Case, Shri Aurobindo became the recognised leader of Hindu cultural nationalism in Bengal.

Significance of 'Bande Mataram' in India's Struggle for Freedom

Unlike European Nationalism, Bankim believed that nationalism was capable of combining nationalism with universal love. His conviction in religion in general and Hindu religion in particular, as the basis of morality, led him to hope that "only Hinduism could bring about a synthesis of nationalism and love for all humanity". His novel 'Anandamath' played a spirited and dynamic part in the awakening of a great Nation. 'Anandamath' was the first Nationalist imagining of the "Nation" as the mother in pre-independence Indian fiction. India's national song, Bande Mataram was first published as a poem in this novel as the rallying cry of the characters that used it to give themselves the courage and to urge people to fight against the British.

The power of Bande Mataram chant inspired equally the Mahatma Gandhi pacifists and the Aurobindo Ghosh revolutionaries. Due to its tradition of sacrifice and its success in bringing a country together against the British, the first two verses of the song were adopted as the National Song of India in October, 1937 by the Congress Working Committee before the end of colonial rule in August, 1947. But the significance of 'Bande Mataram mantra' was not fully recognised in India till the year 1905. In that year, the then Viceroy of India, Lord Curzon, to destroy the solidarity of the people of the then Bengal, partitioned the province of Bengal. The Indians viewed the partition as an attempt by the British to disrupt the growing National Movement in Bengal and divide the Hindus and Muslims of the region. The Bengali Hindu intelligentsia exerted considerable influence on local and national politics. The partition outraged Bengalis. The decision of Bengal partition united India and the great nationalist movement was born in Bengal. 'Bande Mataram' became the inspiration of this revolutionary movement.

Widespread agitation ensued in the streets and the press, and the Congress advocated boycotting British products under the banner of swadeshi. A growing movement emerged focussing on indigenous Indian industries, finance, and education, which saw the founding of the National Council of Education, the birth of Indian financial institutions and banks, as well as an interest in Indian culture and achievements in science and literature. Hindus showed unity by tying Rakhi on each other's wrists and observing Arandhan (not cooking any food). The chief architects of this uncompromising

Swadwshi movement, were Aurobindo Ghosh, Bal Gangadhar Tilak, Bipin Chandra Pal, and Lala Lajpat Rai. It was strongest in Bengal and was also called Bande Mataram Movement in Andhra Pradesh. Bipin Chandra Pal visited Rajahmundry city of Andhra Pradesh in April, 1905 during the Bande Mataram Movement and delivered his speech. Bande Mataram created a national wave throughout the country regardless of age among Indians. Almost 1200 km away from Bengal, at Neel City High School in Nagpur, a brilliant student of 10th grade was expelled for singing Bande Mataram in an agitation he participated; that patriot school student was none other than Dr. Keshav Baliram Hedgewar or 'Doctorji', who established RSS in 1925.

Bande Mataram created a national wave throughout the country regardless of age among Indians. Almost 1200 km away from Bengal, at Neel City High School in Nagpur, a brilliant student of 10th grade was expelled for singing Bande Mataram in an agitation he participated; that patriot school student was none other than Dr. Keshav Baliram Hedgewar or 'Doctorji', who established RSS in 1925.

Shaping of Hindu Polity and Nationalism

In 1902 and 1903, Shri Aurobindo and Sister Nivedita visited Midnapore. They held a series of public lectures and private sessions with the existing revolutionary groups for freedom. Khudiram Bose, a teenager, was an active participant in the discussions about the revolution. He joined Anushilan Samiti and came into contact with the network of Barindra Kumar Ghosh of Calcutta. Khudiram became a volunteer at the age of 15 and was arrested for the attempt to kill Kingsford at Muzaffarpur on 29th April, 1908. The next day, Khudiram Bose was arrested at the then Waini station near Samastipur. On 1 May, the handcuffed Khudiram was brought to Muzaffarpur. The entire town descended at the police station to take a look at the teenage boy surrounded by a team of armed policemen. Khudiram was taken to the house of the district magistrate. The English daily, 'The Statesman', wrote on the following day, 2 May 1908:

The Railway station was crowded to see the boy. A mere boy of 18 or 19 years old, who looked quite determined. He came out of a first-class compartment and walked all the way to the phaeton, kept for him outside, like a cheerful boy who knows no anxiety.....on taking his seat, the boy lustily cried 'Vandemataram'.

Aurobindo was also arrested on charges of planning and overseeing the attack and imprisoned in solitary confinement

in Alipore Jail. The trial of the Alipore Bomb Case lasted for a year, but eventually, he was acquitted on 6 May, 1909. His defence counsel was Chittaranjan Das. It might be a short period but Aurobindo's activity delivered a complete transformation of India's political scene. He became highly influenced by the concept of Tilak's "Swaraj is my birthright" and Bipin Chandra Pal's "complete autonomy" from Britain. However, none went as far as Aurobindo in articulating the legitimacy and necessity of complete independence. He "based his claim for freedom for India on the inherent right to freedom, not on any charge of misgovernment or oppression". He wrote:

"Political freedom is the life-breath of a nation. To attempt social reform, educational reform, industrial expansion, the moral improvement of the race without aiming first and foremost at political freedom, is the very height of ignorance and futility. The primary requisite for national progress, national reform, is the habit of free and healthy national thought and action, which is impossible in a state of servitude."

Aurobindo became inspired by the story of Bankim Chandra Chattopadhyay's novel 'Anandamath' and the writings of Swami Vivekananda. He acknowledged Bankim Chandra as his political guru, as he said:

'Of the new spirit which is leading the nation to resurgence and independence, Bankim Chandra Chatterji is the inspirer and the political guru..."

Aurobindo frequently shared with his younger brother Barin his ideas of imparting martial and intellectual training to the youth of Bengal for the coming revolution; loosely like the sannyasis of Anandamath who stir a rebellion against the British. With the help of his younger brother a journalist, Barindra Kumar Ghosh, he established contacts

with revolutionaries, inspiring patriots such as Bagha Jatin or Jatindranath Mookerjee and Surendranath Tagore. He helped establish a series of youth clubs, including the Anushilan Samiti of Calcutta in 1902. During its existence, the Samiti collaborated with other revolutionary organisations in India and abroad. It was led by nationalists such as Aurobindo Ghosh and his brother Barindra Ghosh and influenced by philosophies as diverse as Hindu Shakta philosophy propounded by Bengali literature of Bankim and Vivekananda. The Samiti was involved in several noted incidences of revolutionary attacks against British interests and administration in India, including the 1912 attempt on the life of the Viceroy of India, and the Seditious conspiracy during World War I led by Rashbehari Bose and Jatindranath Mookerjee respectively. The organisation's political views were expressed in the journal Jugantar, founded in March, 1906 by Abinash Chandra Bhattacharya, Barindra, Bhupendranath Dutt, and Debabrata Basu and a revolutionary organization named Jugantar soon followed. Along with 21 revolutionaries like Surya Sen, Aurobindo Ghosh, Barin Ghosh. Bagha Jatin, Khudiram Bose, Prafulla Chaki, Pritilata Waddedar, Kanailal Dutta, Santosh Kumar Mitra, Ullaskar Dutta, and others- they started to collect arms, explosives and manufactured bombs. Aurobindo provided the ideological foundation to the Jugantar party, as an offshoot of the Anushilan Samiti. Among the operational aims of this society was to sensitize and stimulate the disaffected youth of Bengal to the nationalist cause. In his famous Uttarpara Speech, Aurobindo outlined the essence and the goal of India's nationalist movement:

"I say no longer that nationalism is a creed, a religion, a faith; I say that it is the Sanatan Dharma which for us is nationalism. This Hindu nation was born with the Sanatan Dharma, with

it, it moves and with it, it grows. When the Sanatan Dharma declines, then the nation declines, and if the Sanatan Dharma were capable of perishing, with the Sanatan Dharma it would perish."

In the same speech, he also gave a comprehensive perspective of Hinduism, which is at variance with the geocentric view developed by the later day nationalist ideologues such as Veer Savarkar and Deendayal Upadhyay:

"But what is the Hindu religion? What is this religion which we call Sanatan, eternal? It is the Hindu religion only because the Hindu nation has kept it, because in this Peninsula it grew up in the seclusion of the sea and the Himalayas, because in this sacred and ancient land it was given as a charge to the Aryan race to preserve through the ages. But it is not circumscribed by the confines of a single country, it does not belong peculiarly and forever to a bounded part of the world. That which we call the Hindu religion is really the eternal religion, because it is the universal religion which embraces all others. If a religion is not universal, it cannot be eternal. A narrow religion, a sectarian religion, an exclusive religion can live only for a limited time and a limited purpose. This is the one religion that can triumph over materialism by including and anticipating the discoveries of science and the speculations of philosophy."

Nationalism: Vivekananda and Rabindranath Tagore

Aurobinda Ghosh was deeply inspired by Swami Vivekananda's Nationalism view and Rabindranath felt deeply for Aurobinda Ghosh.

Aurobinda Ghosh was deeply inspired by Swami Vivekananda's Nationalism view and Rabindranath felt deeply for Aurobinda Ghosh.

Nobody can deny their contribution to Bharat Bhumi. Rabindranath has gifted us our National anthem "Jana Gana Mana Adhinayaka Jaya He Bharat Bhagya Vidhata.........". And Swami Vivekananda as a penniless Sannyasi crossed the ocean and made the whole world realise what is India, who strongly believed in a renunciation of the world through path of sannyasa and never became shy about his self-identity as a proud Hindu. According to Vivekananda, religion was the primary source in the formation of National life-current-

You have withstood the shocks of centuries simply because you took great care of it, you sacrificed everything else for it. Your forefathers underwent everything boldly, even death itself, but preserved their religion. Temple after temple was broken down by the foreign conqueror, but no sooner had the wave passed than the spire of the temple rose up again. Some of these old temples of Southern India and those like Somnâth of Gujarat will teach you volumes of wisdom, will give you a keener insight into the history of the race than any amount of books. Mark how these temples bear the marks of a hundred attacks and a hundred regenerations, continually destroyed and continually springing up out of the ruins, rejuvenated and strong as ever! That is the national mind, which is the national life-current. I do not mean to say that political or social improvements are not necessary, but what I mean is this, and I want you to bear it in mind, that they are secondary here and that religion is primary.

> ***The idea of Tagore's nationalism was different than Swamiji's, but nobody can deny their contribution to Bharat Bhumi.***

A Nationalist and a patriot-saint, Swamiji had envisioned the dawn of New India, how and what it should be. According to him, future India would be the proud home not only of the advanced sections of Indian society but also of its backward sections. His success in lifting religion from the abyss of dogmas and giving it a dynamic meaning by linking religion with social service resulted in the building of a new ideology that went a long way towards promoting national unity. Swami Vivekananda stands "For our National welfare," declared Vivekananda, "India must gather up its scattered spiritual forces. India must be a union of those whose hearts beat to the same spiritual tune."

If the modern age Hindu Renaissance in the 19th century was initiated by the Brahmo Samaj movement, then it was overarched by Swami Dayanand Saraswati of the Arya Samaj movement and influenced many political leaders of the Indian Independence movement. But any school of thought or style of action, of Indian Independence movement, was highly inspired by the "patriot prophet" Swami Vivekananda's vision of spiritual nationalism and the concept of the revitalisation of the Hindu Rashtra.

Gandhi and Indian Freedom Struggle:

At the request of Gopal Krishna Gokhale, Gandhi returned to India in 1915 from South Africa. With the help of the moderate group led by Gokhale, Gandhi took leadership of the Congress in 1920. At the Kolkata session of the Congress in September, 1920, Gandhi convinced other leaders of the need to start a non-cooperation movement in support of Khilafat as well as for dominion status. The first Satyagraha movement urged the use of khadi and Indian material as alternatives to those shipped from Britain. It also urged people to boycott British educational institutions and law courts; resign from government employment; refuse to pay taxes, and forsake British titles and honours. The movement enjoyed widespread popular support, and the resulting unparalleled magnitude of disorder presented a serious challenge to foreign rule.

However, Gandhi called off the movement after the deaths of policemen at Chauri Chaura in 1922, because he was scared that India would descend into anarchy. Gandhi was arrested on 10 March, 1922 on sedition charge and sentenced to six years' imprisonment but released in February, 1924. In the meantime, with Gandhi isolated in prison, the Indian National Congress split into two factions. One led by Chittaranjan Das and Motilal Nehru favouring party participation in the legislatures, and the other led by Chakravarti Rajagopalachari and Sardar Vallabhbhai Patel, opposing this move. Meanwhile, in the year 1923, Bose was elected the President of All India Youth Congress and also the Secretary of Bengal State Congress. He was also the editor of the newspaper "Forward", founded by Chittaranjan Das. Bose had been a leader of the younger, revolutionary wing of the Indian National Congress in the late 1920s and 1930s, rising to become Congress President in 1938 and also in 1939 against Gandhi's nominee, Dr. Pattabhi Sitaramayya, but left the Congress when the All-India leaders resigned en masse in protest of his abandonment of the principles introduced by Gandhi.

> ***"the key to his (Gandhi) satyagraha is rooted in the Hindu Upanishad texts" according to William Borman and "Gandhi's ideas on ahimsa and satyagraha were founded on the philosophical foundations of Advaita Vedanta"***

Bose believed that Gandhi's approach of non-violence would never be sufficient to secure India's independence and advocated violent resistance. He was subsequently placed under house arrest by the British, before escaping from India in 1940. The Indian National Congress, the main instrument of Indian nationalism, praised Bose's patriotism but distanced itself from his tactics and ideology. Bose became highly inspired by the Soviet Socialism and Swami Vivekananda's teachings on universalism and on the other hand "the key to his (Gandhi) satyagraha is rooted in the Hindu Upanishad texts" according to William Borman and "Gandhi's ideas on ahimsa and satyagraha were founded on the philosophical foundations of Advaita Vedanta", according to Prof. Indira Carr.

At the age of 57, Gandhi declared himself to be Advaitist Hindu in his religious persuasion but added that he supported Dvaitist viewpoints and religious pluralism. However, some scholars state that the Muslim leaders, who championed the cause of partition and creation of a separate Muslim Pakistan, considered Gandhi to be a Hindu nationalist or revivalist.

□

Hindutva and Nationalism in Bengal

A Historical perspective

The left narrative may love to portray Hindutva's political ambition always remained frustrated in Bengal- as the ideological objective and political milieu in a hostile Communist bastion had never been congenial to its brand of politics. But unfortunately, left intellectuals failed to establish their "Socialist" philosophy in the land of Shri Ramachandra, Shiva, Kali, and Durga. In the land of Shakti and Bhakti Yoga–In the land of 'Bharat Mata' and Neo Vedanta philosophy of Swami Vivekananda and of course in the land of Hindutva. The nationalist tradition is not alien to West Bengal.

> ***The nationalist tradition is not alien to West Bengal. Like most modern ideas in India, "Hindutva," too, was always there in Bengal. Cultural nationalism is the core binding philosophy of a larger Indian nationalism. Nationalism was substantially developed in Bengal, and taken forward later by Tilak and V.D. Savarkar.***

Four texts from the second half of the nineteenth century sculpted different perspectives of the Hindu dharma. These are Rajnarayan Basu's "Hindu Dharmer Sresthattva" ('The Superiority of the Hindu dharma', 1879), Bankim Chandra Chatterjee's "Dharmatattva" (1888, 'Principles of Dharma'), Bhudeb Mukhopadhyay's "Samajik Prabandha" ('Essays on Society', 1892). But the modern historians argue that the term Hindutva or the context of political Hindutva was first mentioned by the literary scholar Chandranath Basu (1844-1910) of the then Bengal province in his work "Hindutva", 1892. According to the noted historian Amiya P. Sen, "To the best of my knowledge, the term Hindutva was first used in modern times by Bangla literary scholar Chandranath Basu (1892) in the work 'Hindutva bā hindur prakr̥ita itihās' (Hindutva or the Authentic History of the Hindus)".

Politics and Bengal

It is not just Syama Prasad Mookerjee but the idea of 'Political Hindutva' shaped in Bengal. The idea of Hindu Rashtra and unified India took shape here in Bengal as well. Also, the Hindu Mahasabha, Bharatiya Jana Sangh, and RSS gained strength and inspiration to form their narrative.

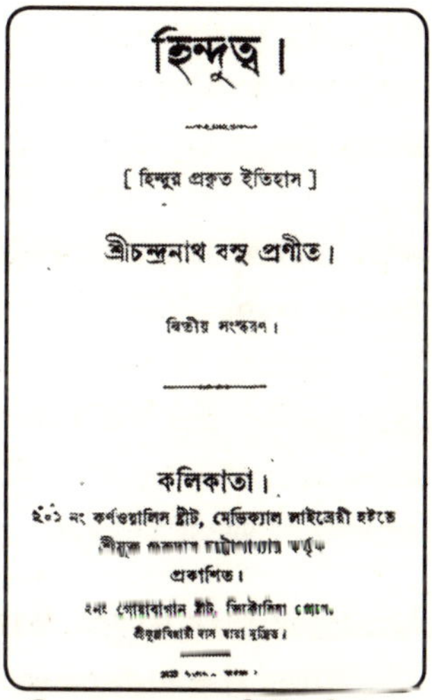
হিন্দুত্ব।

[হিন্দুর প্রকৃত ইতিহাস]

শ্রীচন্দ্রনাথ বসু প্রণীত।

দ্বিতীয় সংস্করণ।

কলিকাতা।

২০১ নং কর্ণওয়ালিস ষ্ট্রীট, মেডিক্যাল লাইব্রেরী হইতে

প্রকাশিত।

Cover page of Hindutva written in Bengali by Chandranath Basu

Rashtriya Swayamsevak Sangh (RSS) founder Dr. Hedgewar's stint as a medical student in Calcutta was greatly influenced by Bengal's nationalists. Honorable Guru ji M.S. Golwalkar's time at the Ramakrishna Math was a factor in his understanding of Nationalism, as one characterised by ideas of service and renunciation. It was on

Dr. Hedgewar and V.D. Savarkar's advice that Syama Prasad Mookerjee became the president of the Hindu Mahasabha, after joining the organisation in 1939 and would later, go on to form the Bharatiya Jana Sangh (BJS), popularly known as the Jana Sangh, merged with several other parties to form the Janata Party after the State of Emergency in 1977; it defeated the incumbent Congress party in the 1977 general election. After three years in power, the Janata party dissolved in 1980 with the members of the erstwhile Jana Sangh reconvening to form the BJP.

Election symbol of Bharatiya Jana Sangh (now BJP) between 1951 and 1977

However, from 1952, when the BJS (Bharatiya Jan Sangh) contested from six of Bengal's 36 seats and won two with a vote share of 5.59%, to 2019, when the BJP contested from 42 seats and won 18 with a vote share of 40%, the Social recognition for Indian Nationalism in the state has come a long way. Throughout this period, the RSS has remained a constant, albeit changing form over the decades. It has been a binding factor among the people of West Bengal.

Mainstream Right Narrative in India

After the independence of India, the Jana Sangh, which was started by Syama Prasad Mookerjee on 21 October, 1951. On the request of Syama Prasad Mookerjee Guru ji loaned several of its leading pracharaks, or full-time workers, to the Jana Sangh to get the new party off the ground. Prominent among these was Deendayal Upadhyay, who was appointed General Secretary. The Jana Sangh's aims included the protection of India's "Hindu" cultural identity, in addition to countering what it perceived to be the appeasement of Muslim people and the country of Pakistan by the Congress party and then-Prime Minister Jawaharlal Nehru. The Jana Sangh's first major campaign, begun in early 1953, centered on demand for the complete integration of Jammu and Kashmir into India. Mookerjee was arrested in May, 1953 for violating orders from the state government restraining him from entering Kashmir. He died the following month, while still in jail.

Lalkrishna Adwani, Atal Vihari Vajpayee and Bhairon Singh Shekhawat

Akhil Bharat Hindu Mahasabha, popularly known as the Hindu Mahasabha was formed to protect the rights of the Hindu community in British India, after the formation of the

> ***The Hindu Mahasabha was founded in 1915 by the noted Indian educationist and politician, Madan Mohon Malaviya. Hindu Mahasabha gained popularity in Bengal in connection with the disputes after the partition of Bengal in 1905 in British India.***

All India Muslim League in 1906 and the British India government's creation of separate Muslim electorate under the Morley-Minto reforms of 1909. The Hindu Mahasabha was founded in 1915 by the noted Indian educationist and politician, Madan Mohon Malaviya. Hindu Mahasabha gained popularity in Bengal in connection with the disputes after the partition of Bengal in 1905 in British India. And in 1947, the then Hindu Mahasabha leader, founder of Jana Sangh, Syama Prasad Mookerjee saved West Bengal by ensuring it did not join Pakistan.

Sawarkar and Dr. Mookerjee

□

Post Independence Crisis in India

Partition Causing Massacre and Misery of Millions

India's independence movement and the Partition in 1947 had its roots in undivided Eastern India. The Muslim League was founded in Dhaka in 1906. In the 1937 provincial elections, it came to power in Bengal in alliance with the Krishak Praja Party. In 1944, it gained an absolute majority in the Bengal Assembly, and Hussein Suhrawardy became the Chief Minister.

On 16 August, 1946, Muhammad Ali Jinnah proclaimed 'Direct Action Day', with the stated goal of peacefully highlighting the demand for a Muslim homeland in British India. That very evening, in Calcutta, Hindus were attacked by Muslim celebrants returning from the then Muslim League's Chief Minister of Bengal province, Huseyn Shaheed Suhrawardy's meeting at 'Shaheed Minar'.

On 16 August, 1946, Muhammad Ali Jinnah proclaimed 'Direct Action Day', with the stated goal of peacefully highlighting the demand for a Muslim homeland in British India. That very evening, in Calcutta, Hindus were attacked by Muslim celebrants returning from the then Muslim League's Chief

Minister of Bengal province, Huseyn Shaheed Suhrawardy's meeting at 'Shaheed Minar'. In his book, 'The Partition of India', Professor Ian Talbot vividly portrayed the attacks on Hindus as "Despite the Muslim League's denials, the outbreak was linked with the celebration of Direct Action Day. Muslim procession that had gone to the staging ground of the 150-foot Ochterlony Monument (Shaheed Minar) on the maidan to hear the Muslim League Prime Minister Suhrawardy, attacked Hindus on their way back. They were heard shouting slogans as 'Larke Lenge Pakistan' (We shall win Pakistan by force). Violence spread to North Calcutta when Muslim crowds tried to force Hindu shopkeepers to observe the day's strike (hartal) call. The circulation of pamphlets in advance of Direct Action Day demonstrated a clear connection between the use of violence and the demand for Pakistan." The next day, Hindus struck back and the violence continued for three days in which approximately 4,000 people died (according to official accounts), Hindus and Muslims in equal numbers.

The Indian National Congress and Gandhi called for the British to Quit India. However, the Muslim League demanded, "Divide and Quit India". He had been outraged by Jinnah's Direct Action campaign, which had provoked communal violence across India, and by the viceroy's vetoes of his home department's plans to stop the violence on the grounds of constitutionality.

Role of Syama Prasad Mookerjee in Bengali Hindu Homeland Movement

The then Hindu Mahasabha leader and the founder of the Bharatiya Jana Sangh, Syama Prasad Mookerjee demanded the partition of Bengal in 1946 to prevent the inclusion of its Hindu-majority areas in a Muslim-dominated East Pakistan.

A meeting held by the Hindu Mahasabha in April 1947, in Tarakeshwar, authorized him to take steps for ensuring the partition of Bengal and this was the beginning of the 'Bengali Hindu Homeland Movement'. According to historian Amalendu De, the partition of Bengal was demanded for the first time by the Bengal Provincial Hindu Mahasabha during the Kolkata riots.

Earlier in February, the Bengal Hindu Sabha constituted a committee for the creation of a separate province for the Hindus of Bengal and began campaigning in the districts. In the first week of April, it convened a three-day-long Bengal Hindu Conference at Tarakeshwar, starting on the 4th and attended by over 400 delegates from all over Bengal and over 50,000 people. In his presidential address on the first day of the conference, the then Hindu Mahasabha leader Nirmal Chandra Chatterjee (father of former Lok Sabha speaker, Somnath Chatterjee) explained that "the reason for demanding partition now, was to sustain nationalism, carve out a separate homeland for the Bengali Hindu people and constitute it as a province within India, and preserve the Bengali culture and heritage". On the same day, on 4th April, the working committee of the Bengal Congress passed a resolution demanding the partition of Bengal. The meeting was attended by Dr. Syama Prasad Mookerjee, Kshitish Chandra Niyogi, Dr. Bidhan Chandra Roy, Nalini Ranjan Sarkar, Dr. Pramathanath Banerjee, Debendra Lal Khan, Makhanlal Sen, and Atul Chandra Gupta among others.

On 5 April, in his speech at the Bengal Hindu Conference at Tarakeshwar, Syama Prasad, suggested the partition of Bengal as the only solution to the communal problem. On the concluding day at the Bengal Hindu Conference at Tarakeswar, authorizing Dr. Syama Prasad Mookerjee to constitute a council of action to establish a separate homeland for the Bengali Hindus. After this, the Bengal Hindu Mahasabha and the Congress intensified their campaigns. No less than 76 Partition meetings were held, of which 59 were convened by the Congress, 12 by the Mahasabha, and five jointly.

On the concluding day at the Bengal Hindu Conference at Tarakeswar, authorizing Dr. Syama Prasad Mookerjee to constitute a council of action to establish a separate homeland for the Bengali Hindus. After this, the Bengal Hindu Mahasabha and the Congress intensified their campaigns. No less than 76 Partition meetings were held, of which 59 were convened by the Congress, 12 by the Mahasabha, and five jointly.

Dr. Syama Prasad Mookerjee further clarified that the movement for the partition of Bengal was not directly related to the partition of India. Even if Pakistan was not created, it was necessary to partition Bengal for the safety of the Bengali Hindu people and their culture.

Syama Prasad roped in the media, including leading newspapers of those times like Dainik Basumati, The Statesman, Amrita Bazar Patrika, and others to campaign for the partition of Bengal. Sajanikanta Das, the editor of 'Shanibarer Chithi', a Bengali weekly noted that the Bengali Hindu Homeland Movement was being led by Dr. Syama Prasad Mookerjee, Major General A.C. Chatterjee, and Dr. Pramathanath Banerjee, therefore one can be rest assured that they would leave no stone unturned to achieve it. On 23 April 1947, Amrita Bazar Patrika published an article titled, 'Homeland for Bengali Hindus', where the results of a gallop poll were published. The survey revealed that an overwhelming 98.3% of the Bengali Hindus wanted the partition of Bengal and the creation of a separate Bengali Hindu homeland. On the next day 24 April, 'The Statesman' commented that the resentment among the middle-class Bengali Hindus towards the Muslim League government was so high that nothing less than Partition would satisfy them. The leading intellectuals like Dr. Ramesh Chandra Majumder, Dr. Makhanlal Raychaudhuri, Dr. Suniti Kumar Chattopadhyay, Pandit Ramshankar Tripathi, Dr. Meghnad Saha, Dr. Jadunath Sarkar supported Syama Prasad Mookerjee and demanded a separate homeland for the Bengali Hindu people on the ground of security. In May 1947, both the Hindu Mahasabha and Congress jointly convened a mammoth public meeting, presided over by historian Dr. Jadunath Sarkar, to press for Partition. The eminent Congress leaders of Bengal, both Kiran Shankar Roy and Dr. Bidhan Chandra Roy assured Dr. Syama Prasad Mookerjee, that they would convince the Congress Working Committee of the need for partition of Bengal.

Muhammad Ali Jinnah realized, Syama Prasad successfully turned and exposed his 'dangerous' tactics, demanding West Bengal for Bengali Hindus and the Congress emphasizing on the partition of Punjab. But by then, Syama Prasad had already met the Viceroy Mountbatten and explained that if the Cabinet Mission Plan failed and British India was to be partitioned, then Bengal should also be partitioned. On 4th May, 1947 Jinnah defended the idea of partition of Bengal and Punjab in his speech at Delhi:

"I should like to point out that there is a great deal of confusion created on purpose. The question of a division of India, as proposed by the Muslim League, is based on the fundamental fact that there are two nations-Hindus and Muslims-and the underlying principle is that we want a national home and a national state in our homelands which are predominately Muslim and comprise the six units of Punjab, the N.W.F.P. (Khyber Pakhtunkhwa), Sind, Baluchistan, Bengal, and Assam. This will give the Hindus their national home and a national state of Hindustan, which means three-fourths of British India....."

Dr. Syama Prasad Mookerjee asserted and argued "If 35 percent of Muslims cannot live in India with 62 percent Hindus, there was no way that 42 percent Hindus can stay in a Bengal with 54 percent Muslims." But the leader of the Indian National Congress, Khan Abdul Ghaffar Khan and Mahatma Gandhi, both strongly opposed the partition of India. Though the ideology of 'the two-nation theory' was that the religion is the determining factor in defining the nationality of Indian Muslims was undertaken by Muhammad Ali Jinnah, who termed it as the awakening of Muslims for the creation of Pakistan. Gandhi suggested an agreement which required the Congress and the Muslim League to co-operate and attain independence under a provisional government, thereafter, the question of partition could be resolved by a plebiscite in the districts with a Muslim majority. Jinnah rejected Gandhi's proposal and called for Direct Action Day, on 16 August 1946, which triggered a mass murder of Calcutta Hindus and the torching of their property, and apathetic police were missing to contain or stop the conflict.

> ***"If 35 percent of Muslims cannot live in India with 62 percent Hindus, there was no way that 42 percent Hindus can stay in a Bengal with 54 percent Muslims."***

Communal violence in Bengal and Punjab in January and March, 1947 further convinced Vallabhbhai Patel of the soundness of partition. Patel, a fierce critic of Jinnah's demand that the Hindu-majority areas of Punjab and Bengal be included in a Muslim state, obtained the partition of those provinces, thus blocking any possibility of their inclusion in Pakistan. Patel's decisiveness on the partition of Punjab and Bengal had won him many supporters and admirers amongst the Indian public, which had tired of the League's tactics, but he was criticized by Gandhi, Nehru, secular Muslims, and socialists for a perceived eagerness to do so.

When Lord Louis Mountbatten formally proposed the plan on 3 June 1947, Vallabhbhai Patel gave his approval and lobbied Nehru and other Congress leaders to accept the proposal. Knowing Gandhi's deep anguish regarding proposals of partition, Patel engaged him in frank discussion in private meetings over the perceived practical unworkability of any Congress-League coalition, the rising violence, and the threat of civil war. At the All India Congress Committee meeting called to vote on the proposal, Patel said:

"I fully appreciate the fears of our brothers from the Muslim-majority areas. Nobody likes the division of India and my heart is heavy. But the choice is between one division and many divisions. We must face facts. We cannot give way to emotionalism and sentimentality. The Working Committee has not acted out of fear. But I am afraid of one thing, that all our toil and hard work of these many years might go waste or prove unfruitful. My nine months in office have completely disillusioned me regarding the supposed merits of the Cabinet Mission Plan. Except for a few honourable exceptions, Muslim officials from the top down to the chaprasis (peons or servants) are working for the League. The communal veto given to the League in the Mission Plan would have blocked India's progress at every stage. Whether we like it or not, de facto Pakistan already exists in the Punjab and Bengal. Under the circumstances, I would prefer a de jure Pakistan, which may make the League more responsible. Freedom is coming. We have 75 to 80 percent of India, which we can make strong with our genius. The League can develop the rest of the country."

After Gandhi rejected and Congress approved–the plan, Patel represented India on the Partition Council, where he oversaw the division of public assets and selected the Indian council of ministers with Nehru. On 20 June 1947, all legislators of the Bengal Legislative Assembly from Hindu-majority areas of the province voted for the partition of Bengal and the creation of (West Bengal), a separate homeland for Bengali Hindus.

On 20 June 1947, all legislators of the Bengal Legislative Assembly from Hindu-majority areas of the province voted for the partition of Bengal and the creation of (West Bengal), a separate homeland for Bengali Hindus.

Religious Persecution and Refugee Overflow: West Bengal Affected the Most

Neither Patel nor any other Indian leader had foreseen the intense violence and population transfer that would take place with partition. Patel took the lead in organizing relief and emergency supplies, establishing refugee camps, and visiting the border areas with Pakistani leaders to encourage peace. Despite these efforts, the death toll is estimated at between 500,000 and 1 million people. The estimated number of refugees in both countries exceeds 15 million.

Millions of Hindus migrated to India from East Bengal. The majority of them settled in West Bengal. A smaller number went to Assam, Tripura and other states. However, the refugee crisis was markedly different from Punjab at India's western border. Punjab witnessed widespread communal riots immediately before partition. As a result, population transfer in Punjab happened almost immediately after the partition as terrified people left their homes from both sides. Within a year, the population exchange was largely complete between East and West Punjab. But in Bengal, violence was not only limited to Kolkata and Noakhali. And hence in Bengal, migration occurred in a much more gradual fashion and continued over the next three decades following partition. Although riots were limited in pre-independence Bengal, the environment was nonetheless communally charged.

While the Muslim majority districts of Murshidabad and Malda were given to India, the Hindu majority district of Khulna and the Buddhist majority, but sparsely populated, Chittagong Hill Tracts were given to Pakistan by the Radcliffe Award. Thousands of Hindus, located in the districts of East Pakistan which were awarded to Pakistan, found themselves being attacked and this religious persecution forced hundreds of thousands of Hindus from East Pakistan (now Bangladesh) to seek refuge in India.

Thousands of Hindus, located in the districts of East Pakistan which were awarded to Pakistan, found themselves being attacked and this religious persecution forced hundreds of thousands of Hindus from East Pakistan (now Bangladesh) to seek refuge in India.

The political climate in Pakistan deteriorated soon after partition and communal violence started to rise. In 1950, severe riots occurred in Barisal and other places in East Pakistan, causing a further exodus of Hindus. Throughout the next two decades, Hindus left East Pakistan whenever communal tensions flared up or the relationship between India and Pakistan deteriorated, as in 1964. The situation of the Hindu minority in East Pakistan reached its worst in the months preceding and during the Bangladesh Liberation War of 1971, when the Pakistani army systematically targeted ethnic Bengalis regardless of religious background as part of 'Operation Searchlight'. Bengali intelligentsia, academics, and Hindus were targeted for the harshest treatment, with significant indiscriminate killing taking place. The 1971 Bangladesh genocide in which 300,000-3,000,000 civilians were killed and roughly 10 million refugees fled to India.

The 1951 census in India recorded 2.523 million refugees from East Pakistan. Among them, 2.061 million settled in West Bengal. The rest went to Assam, Tripura and other states. By 1973, their number reached over 6 million.

In Punjab, the Indian Government anticipated a population transfer and was ready to take proactive measures. Land plots which were evacuated by Muslims were allotted to incoming Hindu and Sikh refugees. The then Congress Government allocated substantial resources for the rehabilitation of refugees in Punjab. In contrast, there was no such planning in the eastern part of the country. Neither Central nor West Bengal State Government anticipated any large-scale population exchange and no coordinated policy was in place to rehabilitate millions of homeless people. The newly independent country had few resources and the Central Government was exhausted in resettling 7 million refugees in Punjab. Instead of providing rehabilitation, the Indian Government tried to stop and even reverse the refugee influx from East Bengal. India and Pakistan signed the Nehru-Liaquat pact in 1950 to stop any further population exchange between West and East Bengal (the then East Pakistan, now Bangladesh). Both countries agreed to take the refugees back and return them their property which they evacuated in their respective countries. But in practice, both countries failed to uphold it. Even after it became clear that refugees were determined not to be sent back, the governments of both countries failed to provide any significant assistance. The Government policy of East Bengal refugee rehabilitation mostly consisted of sending them to 'empty areas', mostly outside West Bengal. One of the most controversial of such schemes was the Government's decision to settle the refugees by force in Dandakaranya, a barren plot of land in central India. Without the Government's assistance, the refugees often settled themselves. Some found jobs in factories. Many took to small businesses and hawking. Numerous refugee colonies sprang up in Nadia, 24 Parganas (North & South), and Kolkata's suburbs.

Radcliffe Line split Bengal, which historically was always a single economic-cultural-ethnic (Bengali-Hindu or Bengali-Muslim) zone, into two-halves. The two-halves were intricately connected. The fertile East produced food and raw materials which the West consumed and the industrialized West produced manufactured goods, which were consumed by the East. This mutually beneficial trade and exchange were severely disrupted by the partition. Rail, road, and water communication routes were severed between the two. Kolkata was the center of Bengal's economic and social development for both Hindus and Muslims. All large industries, military bases, government offices, and most of the institutions of higher education were situated in Kolkata. After partition, West Bengal suffered from a substantial food shortage as the fertile rice-producing districts of Bengal went to the eastern half. The shortage continued throughout the 1950s and 1960s. By 1959, West Bengal faced an annual food shortage of 950,000 tonnes. Hunger marches became a common sight in Kolkata.

Nehru and His Policy on Refugee Crisis Made a Disaster in West Bengal

Jute was the largest industry in Bengal at the time of partition. Radcliffe Line left every single jute mill in West Bengal but four-fifth of the jute producing land in East Bengal. The best quality fiber-yielding breeds of jute were cultivated mostly in East Bengal. India and Pakistan initially went into a trade agreement to import raw jute from East Bengal for West Bengal's mills. However, Pakistan had plans to set up its mills and put restrictions on raw jute export to India. West Bengal's mills faced an acute shortage. The industry faced a crisis. On the other hand, jute farmers in East Bengal were now without a market to sell their produce. Jute export to West Bengal suddenly became an anti-national act for Pakistan. Smuggling of raw jute shot up across the border. However, West Bengal rapidly increased jute production and by mid-to-late 1950s, became largely self-sufficient in jute. West Bengal's paper and leather industry faced similar problems. The paper mills used East Bengal's bamboo and the tanneries consumed leather, also mainly produced in East Bengal. Like jute, lack of raw material pushed these two industries into decline.

Despite center and state governments' best efforts, the pressure of millions of refugees, food shortages, and industrial decline put post-independence West Bengal in a severe crisis. Dr. B. C. Roy's government tried to cope up with the situation by initiating several projects. The government built irrigation networks like DVC and Mayurakshi project, the Durgapur industrial zone, and Salt Lake City. But these failed to arrest West Bengal's decline. West Bengal lost its top place and lagged well behind other Indian states in industrial development. Massive political unrest, strikes, and violence crippled the state throughout the next three decades after partition.

Union Home Minister (The BJP leading) Shri Amit Shah receive huge regionse during his rallies in West Bengal

Shri Amit Shah having Lunch at BJP Karyakarta Shri Manas Sen's Residence in Kolkata

Booth Chalo Abhiyan

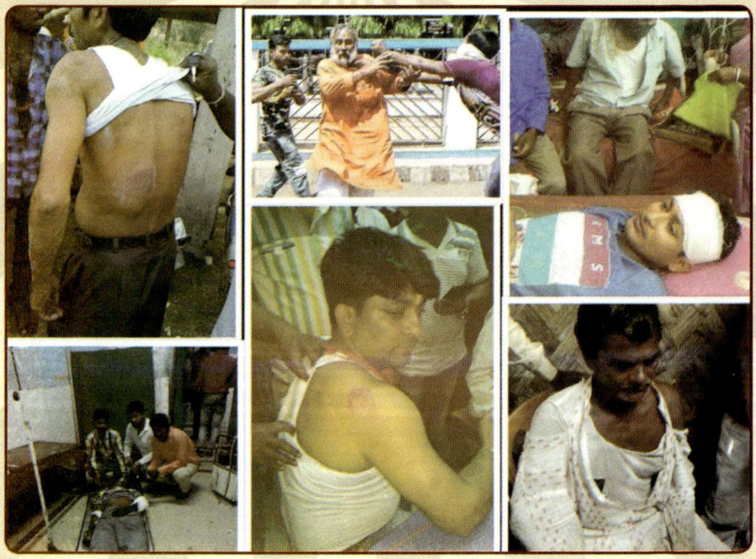

Victims of TMC violence

Dilip Ghosh assuming office of State President

Dilip Ghosh Mukul Roy : Together we shall oust TMC...

RSS passes a resolution on situation and sufferings of Hindus in West Bengal

Mamta Banerjee : Muslim Appeasement

PM Narendra Modiji paying floral tributes to Guruoter Rabindranath Tagore

PM Modi with CM Mamta

Meating of BJP MPs from West Bengal

Printing Kailash

Ram Navami Shobhayatra

BJP President Shri JP Nadda with West Bengal BJP team

Nandigram Violence

Save Bengal Launch

Vistarak Baithak

Some memories may show us the right direction to judge the thought process of Dr. B.C. Roy. It was 1957, when Nehru and P.C. Mahalanobis were all set to introduce Soviet-style planning with an emphasis on creating basic and heavy industries and financing them by curtailing consumption. Roy chose to cross swords with Mahalanobis with his sophisticated econometric models and recommended a policy where the primary emphasis was to be given initially to agriculture. Industrial development was to take place from out of the surplus generated by agriculture. He was opposed to import control or foreign exchange control. But he did not turn his views into polemics and submitted to the majority opinion, when he was overruled by Nehru and Mahalanobis. Nehru might have his compulsion then but one thinks may be, a bit repetition of history, that Gandhi himself advised Dr. Roy to be the Chief Minister of Bengal when Dr. Roy wanted to devote himself to his profession. The West Bengal at that time had been torn by communal violence, shortage of food, unemployment, and a large flow of refugees in the wake of the creation of East Pakistan.

So which factor was mainly responsible for ruining the economic prospects of the states? Here is the much-debated critical question raised by many intellectuals from a different perspective.

Of course, the ruthless and tactical CPI, CPM, and Naxalite movement damaged the economic prospects of the state but that is one of the perspectives to see the whole truth. The incompetent policy of center-left Congress party and immature strategy of left parties on post-independence Bengali Hindu refugees from East Pakistan was highly responsible for the slow death of the State's economy. Moreover in the absence of great personas like Gandhi, Vallabhbhai Patel and Syama

Prasad Mookerjee by 1953, Nehru might be overwhelmed to build the new nation and thus the devastating impact on the industries in Bengal due to partition was not taken care of by the then prime minister of India, Nehru.

This confusing high-drama has been described vividly by the writer and defence analyst Abhijit Bhattacharyya on 25th April, 2001 in the 'Pioneer':

"...In August 1946, Suhrawardy's Direct Action, along with Jinnah's Muslim League, made Partition of India imminent and inevitable. The then Congress leaders of India, too, smelling power, resorted to sweet talks with Hindu Bengalis of East Bengal with vague promises and assurances (to be forgotten in the future, of course) in the event the Muslim League made their existence impossible in East Bengal. The credulous Hindu Bengalis, trapped by the Congress's promise and tripped by the Muslim League's Noakhali violence, voted for Partition.

The rest, as they say, is history -a history of sordid discrimination adopted by all against the Hindu refugees from the East. Nehru's letter of December 2, 1949, to B.C. Roy, says it all: "I do not know what the expenditure incurred on relief and rehabilitation has been for those coming from East Pakistan. Probably you are right in saying that it has been less than that for refugees from West Pakistan. In East Pakistan, the migration has been at a slower pace and rather gradual. In West Pakistan, practically all Hindus or Sikhs were driven out. In East Pakistan, a very large number remained and it was your policy and ours not to do anything which might bring about a wholesale migration to West Bengal from East Pakistan."

Nehru was unashamed to write that he did not know of even the approximate expenditure incurred for the Hindu Bengali refugees of the East. His knowledge revolved around the word "probably", and he did not even care to find out the facts. Nehru's logic was simple - Hindu migration from East Pakistan was undesirable as its continuance would inflict an unmitigated disaster on the Indian economy........"

For the settlement of the refugees, Dr. B. C. Roy thought of the Andaman and Nicobar Islands. It was practically a virgin island ready to welcome human settlement. If the refugees could be sent and settled there, the problem of rehabilitating them could be solved without straining the economy of West Bengal which had been badly hurt by partition. But the myopic leadership of the Left frustrated his effort by insisting that all the refugees are settled in Bengal and none would be allowed to be sent across *kalapani*.

Later, much later, the Left leaders realized their folly. Dandakaranya came up. Some refugees were also sent to the Andamans. There was no resistance. But by then, West Bengal had lost the advantage of taking the initiative.

Nehruvian Model of Development: Gloomy Situation of Bengal, Created a Room for Left Movement in Bengal

According to pro-Neheruvian narrative-During Nehru's three 5-year plans (1951–1965), India's industrial sector would grow at 7.1 percent a year, the number of consumer-goods industries would increase by 70 percent, the production of intermediate goods would quadruple, and the output of capital goods would increase tenfold. India went from a situation where 90 percent of its industrial goods were imported to halving that in 1960 and having only 9 percent of its goods come from abroad in 1974. This form of economic autonomy freed India from the industrialized countries and strengthened its position as a non-aligned country.

Nehru was influenced heavily by the Western yardstick of

development and progress, which was opposite to Gandhian ideology. Gandhi's view was to reinvigorate the village industry, whereby there would be many smaller entrepreneurs making goods from start-to-finish and using local materials, thus in a more traditional and eco-friendly manner. Also, the local economy would be stronger and regional specialities would flourish. But Nehru's admiration for the socialist model of central economic planning and the then absence of a strong private sector, compelled government investment in basic industries and infrastructure. Nehru or Nehruvian school of thought might think that by developing the basic infrastructure of India, they would accomplish development in agriculture as reflected in the early industrial policies. But in the event of doing so, they forgot to develop manufacturing industries in India. While China followed the Gandhian model of developing small scale industries first and then expanding the benefits at the grass root level to the other big manufacturing industries, India focused more on industrialization in agriculture and basic infrastructure development in a rather top to bottom approach. Due to lack of experience and some negligence on part of the early political class and due to the pressure created by the industrial lobby, the policies could only favour the big players and failed to reach the poor farmers.

In Bengal, it appeared an era (1948–1965) of hope and reconstruction. Following the Nehruvian model of development of new industries like Durgapur Steel Plant and Durgapur town came up, the Damodar Valley Corporation power station started functioning and a dairy-based industry came up in Kalyani. But a research study of Jadavpur University shows a gloomy situation of Bengal's economic prospect:

"By 1964, factories in Bombay employed 13.53 lakh people, when West Bengal employed 8.87 lakh people. By 1966, the

number of licenses approved for Maharashtra was higher than that of West Bengal, although the latter was second in India".

"During the next period (1966–76), West Bengal's relative position began to decline further. The Centre's policy of freight equalization gave a "major blow" to the engineering industry of the state. While the central government tried to protect the industries based on the domestic market through import tariffs, it did very little to promote export-oriented industries like jute and tea, which were the traditional industries of West Bengal".

"The state's agriculture during this period was showing very little growth. Between 1952–53 and 1964–65, Tamil Nadu's agricultural growth rate grew by 4.17 percent and West Bengal's by 1.94 percent".

> ***Due to decline in employment between 1965 and 1970, labour unrest began. The situation became worse with crop failure and inflation. Food riots took place and Bengal witnessed the ultra-Left Naxalite movement.***

Due to decline in employment between 1965 and 1970, labour unrest began. The situation became worse with crop failure and inflation. Food riots took place and Bengal witnessed the ultra-Left Naxalite movement. On 18 May 1967, the Siliguri Kishan Sabha, of which Jangal Santhal was the president, declared their support for the movement initiated by Kanu Sanyal, and their readiness to adopt armed struggle to redistribute land to the landless. Around 1971, the Naxalites gained a strong presence among the radical sections of the student movement in Calcutta. Charu Majumdar declared an "annihilation line", a dictum that Naxalites should assassinate individual "class enemies" (such as landlords, businessmen, university teachers, police officers, politicians of the right and left) and others.

The then chief minister of West Bengal, Siddhartha Shankar Ray of the Congress Party, instituted strong counter-measures against the Naxalites. The West Bengal police fought back to stop the Naxalites. In July 1971, Indira Gandhi took advantage of President's rule to mobilize the Indian Army against the Naxalites and launched a colossal combined army and police counter-insurgency operation, termed "Operation Steeplechase," killing hundreds of Naxalites and imprisoning more than 20,000 suspects and cadres, including senior leaders. In 1972, Charu Majumdar was arrested by the police and died in Alipore Jail but CPI(M) emerged as the principal opposition party in West Bengal.

□

The Era of Autocracy 1972–2011

'Black' period of Indian Democracy

In the elections held for State assemblies across India in March 1972, the Congress (R) swept to power in most states riding on the post-war (Bangladesh War) "Indira wave". But Mrs. Gandhi could not even imagine that along with strong opposition of Jayaprakash Narayan and Morarji Desai, a verdict of the Supreme Court would turn the table of power game. On 24 June, 1975 in the Supreme Court of India, Justice V.R. Krishna Iyer, upheld the Allahabad High Court judgment and ordered all privileges Gandhi received as an MP be stopped, and that she be debarred from voting. The next day, JP organized a large rally in Delhi, where he said that a police officer must reject the orders of government if the order is immoral and unethical as this was Mahatma Gandhi's motto during the freedom struggle. Later that day, Indira Gandhi requested a compliant President Fakhruddin Ali Ahmed to proclaim a state of emergency. Within three hours, the electricity to all major newspaper offices was cut and the political opposition arrested. The proposal was sent without discussion to the Union Cabinet, who only learned of it and ratified it the next morning.

Invoking Article 352 of the Indian Constitution, Indira

Gandhi granted herself extraordinary powers and launched a massive crackdown on civil liberties and political opposition. The Government used police forces across the country to place thousands of protestors and strike leaders under preventive detention. Vijayaraje Scindia, Jayaprakash Narayan, Raj Narain, Morarji Desai, Charan Singh, Jivatram Kripalani, Atal Bihari Vajpayee, Lal Krishna Advani, Arun Jaitley, and other protest leaders were immediately arrested. Organizations like the Rashtriya Swayamsevak Sangh (RSS) and Jamaat-e-Islami, along with some political parties, were banned. The RSS, later on, defied the ban and thousands participated in 'Satyagraha' against the ban and the curtailment of fundamental rights. Later, when there was no letup, the volunteers of the RSS formed underground movements for the restoration of democracy. Literature that was censored in the media was clandestinely published and distributed on a large scale and funds were collected for the movement. Networks were established between leaders of different political parties in the jails and outside for the co-ordination of the movement.

'The Economist' described the movement as "the only non-left revolutionary force in the world". It said that the movement was "dominated by tens of thousands of RSS cadres, though more and more young recruits are coming". Talking about its objectives, it said, "its platform at the moment has only one plank: to bring democracy back to India".

When the State of Emergency was lifted and new elections called in 1977, opposition political parties such as the Congress (O), Bharatiya Jana Sangh, Bharatiya Lok Dal as well as 2 defectors from the Congress (R) joined to form the Janata Party, which won a sweeping majority in the Indian Parliament.

In Bengal, at the time of emergency, Jyoti Basu was able to avoid the arrest and went underground with many of his colleagues. Some non-left critics believed it was an understanding between the communists and Indira Gandhi and Communists tacitly supported the Emergency. But Jyoti Basu strongly denounced the allegation and said "There cannot be a bigger lie than this. This is absolutely rubbish. ..."

Though the Communist Party of India was allied with the Congress party during the period 1970–77 in Kerala.

Beginning of Communist Regime and Marichjhapi Genocide: Murder of thousands of Hindu Dalits

In the 1977 West Bengal Legislative Assembly elections, seat-sharing talks between the Left Front and the Janata Party broke down. The Left Front, headed by the Communist Party of India (Marxist), won 243 seats, thereby gaining a majority. The first Left Front government was established with Jyoti Basu as the Chief Minister.

In the initial phase of Left Front governance, two key priorities were land reform and decentralization of administration. Through Operation Barga, in which share-croppers were given inheritable rights on lands they tilled, 1.1 million acres of land were distributed amongst 1.4 million share-croppers. On 4 June, 1978, three-tier panchayat local bodies were elected across the state, elections in which the Left Front won a landslide victory. Some 800,000 acres of land were distributed to 1.5 million heads of households between 1978 and 1982. But surprisingly, their ruthless policy against the Bengali Hindu refugees was very much similar to the 'Socialist Prime Minister' Nehru.

On 31 January, 1979, the CPI(M)-led Left Front government, trained its guns on thousands of Bengali Hindu, mostly Dalits, refugees in 'Marichjhapi', an uninhabited island of Sundarban. In the middle of 1978, around 1.5 lakh Bengali Hindu refugees started settling in Marichjhapi from the refugee camps in Dandakaranya. Most of them were Namasudras, the largest Hindu Dalit caste in Bengal. Driven out by the Islamists in Bangladesh, these Hindu refugees had crossed the border in search of a new home. During their stay in Dandakaranya, the Left—then in Opposition—had promised them that they would be welcomed in once it comes to power.

An approximately 150,000, almost all of Dandakaranya refugees arrived; most of them were deported back. Meanwhile, approximately 40,000 refugees went south and camping for few months in Hasnabad, settled in Marichjhapi (renamed by them as "Netaji Nagar"), a protected place under Reserve Forest Act. But the Left Front meanwhile changed its policy on refugees settling and considered the refugees as a burden to the state, as the refugees were not the citizens of West Bengal, but India. In January 1979, the Jyoti Basu government clamped an economic blockade on the island. For a fortnight, Marichjhapi settlers cried out desperately for food, medicines, and other essentials. Many died of starvation and diseases. Thirty police launches started patrolling the island in February 1979, preventing anyone from providing food or water to the residents of the island. The Calcutta High Court passed an injunction order, asking the government to lift the blockade. Even as the case was pending in High Court, West Bengal police, along with CPI(M) cadres, unleashed unimaginable violence on Marichjhapi on May 14. Trapped and helpless people were butchered; even babies were not spared; women were dragged out of homes and raped. In an overnight operation, around 6,000 huts were set on fire. The report says they took the islanders as prisoners, shot them in the head, put them in sacks, tied them to rocks, and dropped them deep into the river.

On May 17, 1979, Buddhadeb Bhattacharjee, the then State Information Minister, declared at Writers Building that Marichjhapi has been cleared of refugees. The death toll was at least 10,000, even as a government estimate came out with figures as low as 10. The massacre was never investigated.

The Communists continued their violence again on 30 April, 1982, killing and burning 16 Hindu monks and a nun belonging to Ananda Marga at Bijon Setu, near Ballygunge, Kolkata in West Bengal. No arrests were ever made. After repeated calls for a formal judicial investigation, a single-member judicial commission was set up to investigate the killings in 2012.

Poor became Poorer in Bengal's Communist Regime

During the Communist regime in Bengal, industry fled from the state, farm growth tapered off, and Bengal's poor became worse off than poor. Over the years, the Left wrecked public health and public education, neglected bureaucratic proficiency, and paid little heed to the idea of developing infrastructure, technology, and political violence became endemic. In 2007, the National Sample Survey (NSS) found that nearly 11% of families in Bengal faced starvation during several months of the year, the highest among any state in India. A proud party which followed the Soviet Stalinist style in Bengal was responsible for many documented records of atrocities against the poor farmers or sharecroppers or tea garden workers, who belonged to Hindus-Dalits and indigenous (Adivasi) community of 'Jungalmahal' (the border area between Medinipur and Jharkhand) and North Bengal.

Nandigram Violence: A turning point

Land reform policy for the poor peasants was the key factor for the left to come in power in West Bengal but after 34 long years, they lost their regime because of their policy of land acquisition from poor farmers. On 14th March, 2007, "Nandigram was Stalinised the same way Stalin had Siberia-ised Soviet Russia, and justified it too", as Tarun Vijay, the then editor of 'Panchjanya' said. The communist Chief Minister Buddhadeb Bhattacharya's 'Stalinist' move was fiercely countered by other ruthless communist factions, the killer Maoists and Naxals and Leninists – both (Stalinist and Maoist) have "same allergy and hate for Gandhi and Subhas" and "they show the utmost respect for Che Guevara and Fidel Castro". –Mamata Bandopadhyay, the then opposition leader with limited organization in Bengal, took the advantage. An overground and imaginatively named organization flourished at 'Lalgarh', Jhargram and supported by the Maoists, People's Committee Against Police Atrocities (PCAPA), and their local star Chatradhar Mahato were partners with the Trinamool against the CPM as their common enemy. Some critics argued they were Left degenerates, not Maoists. Mamata also managed to test a noticeable 'piece of cake' from Stalinist's vote share as the former CM of Bengal was not in favour of the Salim SEZ at Nandigram. After Nandigram violence in March 2007, for the first time, CPI(M)'s Front allies RSP, CPI and Forward Bloc threatened to walk out of the government. Later on, 'Communists' from all major left parties (Stalinists), joined hands with Trinamool Congress to keep their political power and resources intact.

However, in 2019, twelve years after the anti-land acquisition movement changed the political landscape of West Bengal when the three-decade-long Left rule ended and the Mamata led TMC came to power, many locals in the cradle of change, Nandigram, feel "disenchanted and forgotten" and are craving for another change.

□

Mamata Came in Power with a Populist Slogan of 'Parivartan'

Mamata: the other face of Left

In 2011, the people of West Bengal wanted to get rid of communist atrocities for stable economic development. Mamata longed for years to come in power, fulfilled in 2011, ousting the communist regime of 34 years. But her administrative failure and replicating the political violence of left rulers, she made herself very unpopular within 5 years.

Mamata Banerjee became involved with politics when she was only 15. While studying at the Jogamaya Devi College, she established Chhatra Parishad Union, the student's wing of the Congress (I) Party. Banerjee began her political career in the Congress party as a young woman in the 1970s. A street-fighter and emotional leader, Banerjee first pulled the limelight by blocking Jayaprakash Narayan's convoy by throwing herself on the ground when JP came to Kolkata to organise the mass sentiment against Indira Gandhi before Emergency.

In the 1984 general election, Banerjee became one of India's youngest parliamentarians ever, defeating veteran Communist politician Somnath Chatterjee, to win the Jadavpur parliamentary Constituency in West Bengal. Banerjee was appointed the Union Minister of State in 1991 by Prime Minister P.V. Narasimha Rao. But in 1996, she left the Congress, calling it a 'stooge of CPI(M)' in Bengal. Two years later, she formed the Trinamool Congress along with the then TMC leader Mukul Roy and quickly emerged as a principal opposition party in West Bengal.

How Mamata used BJP-RSS for her own rise

In April, 2019, Mamata Bandopadhyay claimed, "RSS helping Congress in Bengal". She accused Congress of taking the help of the Rashtriya Swayamsevak Sangh (RSS) to defeat Trinamool Congress in Bengal. But Mamata herself asked the RSS to lend her support to oust the Left parties in West Bengal on 15th September, 2003. India's leading newspaper "The Telegraph" reported the event as "Mamata Banerjee today appeared to shed her antipathy towards the Sangh Parivar brand of politics even as a flattered RSS hailed her as Bengal's Durga. The Trinamool Congress chief, who is still without a portfolio, was seeking the Sangh's support in her fight against communist "terror". "If you (the RSS) give us just 1 percent support, we will be able to fight red terror," she told the assembled RSS mass, including H.V. Seshadri, Mohan Bhagwat, and Madan Das Devi. "I have never got to meet so many RSS leaders, though I have met some individually. You people are true patriots. I know you love the country, you care for even small, remote areas of the country," she added."

India's leading newspaper "The Telegraph" reported the event as "Mamata Banerjee today appeared to shed her antipathy towards the Sangh Parivar brand of politics even as a flattered RSS hailed her as Bengal's Durga.

It was at Delhi where Mamata Banerjee went to release a

book, 'Communist Terrorism', compiled and edited by Tarun Vijay, the editor of RSS mouthpiece 'Panchjanya'.

Mamata Banerjee, who started her career in the Congress and formed her party in 1997, had joined the NDA two years later. She became a minister in the NDA governments led by Atal Bihari Vajpayee, holding the railways and the coal and mines portfolios. In 2001, she quit the NDA as a railway minister and fought the assembly election with the Congress but could not make any scratch even against the Left. Immediately afterwords a frustrated Banerjee joined hands with NDA again and become coal and mines minister in Vajpayee cabinet in 2004.

"Her preferred form of conducting politics has been violence. Although the Left Front cadres, too, had historically been prone to serial violence, the critical difference between the Left Front and Mamata was that the Left Front never allowed the RSS-BJP to grow deep roots in the state. In her thirst for power, Mamata not only allowed that but actively welcomed the RSS-BJP to spread across West Bengal...." National Herald, 10 July 2017. But she started Muslim appeasement for the vote bank politics immediately after capturing the power of West Bengal.

Mamata flip-flopped on Illegal Bangladeshi Infiltration

According to the record, she did not have any ideology but often changed her narrative to gain political advantage. On 4 August, 2006, Banerjee hurled her resignation papers at the deputy speaker Charanjit Singh Atwal in Lok Sabha. She was provoked by Speaker Somnath Chatterjee's rejection of her adjournment motion on illegal infiltration by Bangladeshis in West Bengal. Then she was in opposition in West Bengal but almost after 12 years in 2018, she had propagated entirely different stance on the same issue as the Chief Minister of West Bengal. Mamata has been a vocal critic of NRC and has vehemently opposed it. In 2006, he criticized CPI(M) govt on the ground of illegal Bangladeshi infiltration but now they (Bengali speaking Bangladeshi Muslims) may be her most 'trusted' vote bank. Despite the strong anti-incumbency wave, 26 percent of Bengal's 30 percent Muslim population voted for the TMC in the 2019 Lok Sabha poll. "This chunk mostly consists of Bengali-speaking Muslims. A substantial number of them could be from Bangladesh," says Mohit Ray, former professor of Jadavpur University and head of the BJP's refugee cell in the state.

Left lost the Power. Mamata lost the trust

The Left Front came to power in West Bengal on the issue of land in 1977-land reform and the registration of sharecroppers. Ironically, three decades later, its collapse was triggered by a land-related issue-land acquisition for industry took its toll in terms of human lives and the livelihoods of displaced farmers, and snuffed out dreams of industrialization in Nandigam and Singur. But by then, de-industrialization and flight of capital due to misguided government policies had created an alarming unemployment problem; and the erosion of various civic and educational institutions due to political interference had created a widespread hunger for change.

The TMC led by firebrand leader Mamata Banerjee rode to power in 2011 on the plank of parivartan (change), promising corruption-free governance and a revival of the state economy by attracting investment, both domestic and international. But in the 2016 assembly elections, ironically the main election issue that emerged was corruption by the local TMC partymen, Saradha chit fund scandal, and the Narada sting operation.

The vital question is after the 2011 assembly election, has there been any change in the economic scenario of the state under the TMC government? According to the per capita income, if we restrict our attention to the 19 major states with a population of 1 Cr or more, West Bengal's rank was 11th in 2011. In 2014, the rank remains the same. On February 4, 2019, the West Bengal state finance minister had claimed in his Budget speech that West Bengal has attained the top position among all states by securing 16% GSDP growth at current prices in 2017–18. However, there are strong differences of opinion on this claim. According to the Marxist author and economist, Prasenjit Bose, "However, the actual economic growth data that matters is the GSDP at constant prices, which adjusts for inflation. In terms of constant prices, the same CSO data shows GSDP growth to be 9.1% in 2017–18, which means inflation was around 7% in West Bengal, much above the national average".

Divergent Estimates of West Bengal's GSDP Growth Rate at Constant Prices (2011–12 Series)

	GSDP (Constant) Growth % WB Budget 2018–19	GSDP (Constant) Growth %–CSO
2012-13	5.6	4.2
2013-14	6.5	3.0
2014-15	9.0	2.8
2015-16	5.9	6.1
2016-17	8.0	7.9
2017-18	11.5	9.1

Source: Ministry of Statistics & Programme Implementation and Medium Term Fiscal Policy & Fiscal Policy Strategy Statement, 2018–19.

The available evidence, therefore, points to a very little indication of 'parivartan'. The real problem seems tc be that both the Left and the TMC have focused on redistribution, paying little attention to income generation. The expert says, the problem with redistribution without income generation is that in the end, it is a zero-sum game, not very different from Ponzi-schemes like the Saradha. "The government has performed "poorly", as stated in the West Bengal Survey Report 2018, conducted by the West Bengal Election Watch (WBEW) and the Association for Democratic Reforms (ADR) on 'Governance issues and Voting Behaviour 2018', rcleased in April, 2019. The report said the West Bengal government has performed "poorly" in almost all governance issues, mainly on providing better employment opportunities, agriculture loan availability, and higher price realisation for farm products. The survey, which was conducted between October-December 2018, covered 534 parliamentary constituencies and more than 2.37 lakh voters.

The advent of the TMC-led government has seen much confusion regarding its industrial and land acquisition policy. The TMC government has made it clear that it will not acquire any land from the farmers to set up industry and that those interested in setting up industries will have to purchase land directly from the landowners. Questions regarding the feasibility of direct land purchases by corporates in a landscape dominated by many small landholders owning tiny parcels of land have been raised by many. The larger problem remains that the TMC-led government does not have any clear alternative agenda for industrial development.

As the Lok Sabha election 2019 ended, years after their agitation led Tata group to shift the Nano manufacturing plant out of West Bengal and they got their land back, farmers in Singur felt betrayed as the returned plots are non-cultivable and the town does not have enough jobs for them. In 2018, the farmers of Singur undertook a march to Kolkata to demand setting up of industries in the region, said they were "used" by political parties. Singur, in Hooghly Lok Sabha constituency, came to national media attention in 2006-07 amid an anti-land acquisition movement against the Left Front government. The Singur farmers' agitation culminated with the end of 34-year-old Left rule in West Bengal and the Mamata Banerjee-led TMC, which was at the forefront of the protests, coming to power. According to BJP MP from Hoogly, Locket Chatterjee, "TMC has used the poor farmers for their political advantage. If we come to power and the BJP wins from this seat, we must help to bring industries for employment generation in this area".

Mamata Banerjee's decline began with the panchayat elections in 2018. The elections were so undemocratic and violent that in one-third of seats, the winners won unopposed. Nobody dared to contest against them. Media reports suggest that nearly 50 people died during these elections. TMC's Rajya Sabha MP, Derek O'Brien in a tweet said: "To all 'newborn' experts on Bengal #Panchayat Elections in State have a history. 400 killed in poll violence in the 1990s in CPI(M) rule. 2003: 40 dead. Every death is a tragedy. Now closer to normal than earlier times. Yes, a few dozen incidents. Say, 40 out of 58,000 booths. What's % age? " On May 14, 2018, West Bengal's scheduled panchayat polls turned into a bloody affair. Widespread violence had ripped through North and South 24 Parganas, East Midnapore, Burdwan, Nadia, Murshidabad, and South Dinajpur districts as the polling progressed. Crude bombs were hurled, guns were fired, and even police officers and journalists were attacked. This happened after more than 60,000 security personnel were deployed across the state for the panchayat polls. Despite a brutal attack and violence on BJP workers by TMC goons, the BJP won 644 of the 1,944-gram panchayat seats in Purulia, and 329 of the 806 seats in Jhargram. More significantly, the TMC lost 28-gram panchayats out of 79 in Jhargram. The BJP won a total of 5,747-gram panchayats followed by Left Front's 1,708 and Congress's 1,062.

Mamata Banerjee's greatest failure has been the inability to re-imagine a new way of doing politics in West Bengal. Winning a thumping majority for a second consecutive term in 2016, Mamata Banerjee did not feel the need to unlearn the CPM's way of running the state. She used the means and methods of the Left Front to defeat it after 34 years of its uninterrupted rule but followed and continued the communist way of violence which showed the limitations of her political thought.

□

The Beginning of 'Modi Wave' 2014

'Brand BJP' Become Popular in Bengal

In 2014, historic election victory for Modi Bharatiya Janata Party transformed the political landscape of the world's largest democracy of India. The BJP, led by its prime ministerial candidate Narendra Modi, won the Lok Sabha elections, with 282 seats on its own. The alliance it leads—National Democratic Alliance (NDA)—has 336 seats in the lower house of the Parliament. This is the highest number of seats won by any party on its own since the 1984 Lok Sabha elections, when the Congress, led by then Prime Minister Rajiv Gandhi won a landslide victory.

In 2014, Modi ended the coalition era and changed the chemistry of the Indian election. The primary reason Narendra Modi managed to get a massive victory for the BJP was that the people of India desired for a strong 'Leader' over the abstract (Party) 'Ideology'. In 2014, Modi's mammoth win shocked many political pundits who later blamed it as the brilliant marketing of the Modi brand. But in reality, it was not about brand or marketing but the lack of good governance for ten years. There was not a single leader as big, as national as Modi. Congress party was not confident enough to put Rahul Gandhi as the 'leader of India'. The Third front had no product of its own. They wanted people to vote for different leaders in different states and left the question of leadership unanswered. But Modi was visible everywhere in the country. He kicked off his Prime Ministerial campaign from Haryana's Rewari and after that, from TV to rallies to tea sessions to 3D avatars– Modi was everywhere. He said to the people–'candidates do not matter, as long as you vote for BJP, you would vote for me'. He changed the old game and he won the game because he was contesting alone. The ones who understood these 'new rules of the game'- managed to save themselves.

The other winners in the 2014 election were Mamata Banerjee, Jayalalithaa, and Naveen Patnaik. They also wanted votes for themselves without any mixed message and confusion. At the end of the 2014 election, Mamata Banerjee's TMC won 34 seats with 39.05% vote share (+8.13%) and the BJP got 2 seats with a jump of the vote share from 6.14% to 17.02% in West Bengal. But within the next two years, the BJP become the principal opposition party to challenge the citadel of Mamata Banerjee.

Shah Sent A 'Silent Warrior' for the 'Bengal Mission 2016'

Immediately after the 2014 Lok Sabha election results were declared on 16 May, Amit Shah started his preparation for the 2019 election. He planned to expand the organization most effectively. On 7th July, 2014, RSS loaned two of its key functionaries to the Bharatiya Janata Party. One of them was Ram Madhav, the then Akhil Bharatiya Sah-Sampark Pramukh (RSS spokesman) and the other man was Shiv Prakash the then Sangh Kshetra Pracharak of Western Uttar Pradesh and Uttrakhand, highly regarded in the Sangh Parivar for his grassroot work.

Amit Shah became the party president on 9th July 2014. In August, he announced his new team of office-bearers. BL Santosh, Satish Velankar, Saudan Singh, Shiv Prakash Singh and became new joint secretaries (organization). In 2015, BJP President Amit Shah sent 47-year-old Shiv Prakash, joint general secretary (organization), to implement West Bengal 'Mission 2016'. Shiv Prakash had closely worked with Shah in Uttar Pradesh during the 2014 Lok Sabha election and was one of the "Seven Samurai" of Modi 's battle for 2014.

In 2015, BJP President Amit Shah sent 47-year-old Shiv Prakash, joint general secretary (organization), to implement West Bengal 'Mission 2016'. Shiv Prakash had closely worked with Shah in Uttar Pradesh during the 2014 Lok Sabha election and was one of the "Seven Samurai" of Modi 's battle for 2014.

A Silent Saffron Experiment at Baishnabnagar constituency on Indian Muslims 2016

At the time when Mamata enjoyed a 44 percent vote share, people were beginning to associate her party leaders with extortion and infringing on people's democratic rights. The TMC had won the 2016 assembly poll with a two-thirds majority, despite allegations of corruption against its leaders in the Saradha and Rose Valley Ponzi schemes. "The situation was explosive against the ruling party. But BJP could not make use of it, as hardly anyone in rural Bengal dared to hoist a BJP flag atop his house," as the political analysts believed.

The CPIM-led Left Front and Congress, which had allied to fight TMC, failed to put up a creditable performance. TMC got 211 of the 294 seats, bettering its 2011 tally of 184 seats.

In 2011, the TMC-Congress combine had got 48.54% vote share with TMC at 38.9% vote share and the combined vote share of the Left Front was 41%. It's the simple arithmetic of vote share that got the Left Front and the Congress together in the 2016 election. But mathematics did not work. CPIM's vote percentage fell to 19.7% from 29.58% in the 2011 Assembly election and 23% vote share in the 2014 Lok Sabha poll. Congress, however, bettered its vote percentage to 12.3% compared to 8.91% in 2011. BJP, on the other hand, increased its vote percentage to 10.16% compared to 4.06% secured in the 2011 Assembly election and managed to capture three seats for the first time on its own in the state. In the 2016 Assembly polls, BJP has not only secured 56 lakh votes, up from 19.5 lakh in 2011, but it has also made its presence felt in 262 out of 294 Assembly segments where the saffron party polled more than 10,000 votes and a brilliant political experiment silently executed by BJP, with the careful supervision of joint general secretary (organization), Shiv Prakash Singh.

Despite Trinamool Congress' landslide win in the 2016 state polls, Muslim-dominated Malda district continued to be Mamata Banerjee's weakest penetration. Among the 12 Assembly constituencies in Malda, Trinamool could not win even a single seat. While the Congress-CPM alliance won 11 seats and for the first time, the BJP emerged victorious from Baishnabnagar constituency. BJP got a total of 3 seats in 2016, one at Madarihat constituency of Alipurduar, other at Kharagpur Sadar constituency of West Medinipur but BJP's biggest success in Bengal was in the Congress stronghold of Malda, where it won Baishnabnagar constituency dominated by Muslims, which is perhaps a perfect fit for a 'case study' by the saffron brigade. According to BJP, Baishnabnagar was an experiment that they had been doing in Assam, which appeared to be a 'success story' for the BJP.

In the 2016 West Bengal Assembly Election, Baishnabnagar constituency was won by BJP candidate Swadhin Kumar Sarkar with a vote share of 38.20 percent. The vote share of BJP had gone up by 24.12 percent in the area. The constituency includes the Kaliachak block of Malda (West Bengal)-which is widely known for FICN (Fake Indian currency notes), cattle and arms smuggling. The area had a Muslim population of around 52 percent (2016), and it is known as the corridor of Bangladeshi infiltrators.

Just after the 'Kaliachak violence' on 3rd January, 2016, the BJP started organizational work in Baishnabnagar constituency. Then BJP had around 12 to 14 percent votes in the area. In 2016, BJP sensed "Indian Muslims never support anti-national activities. Baishnabnagar is the classic example of getting Indian Muslims on the BJP side" said Siddharth Nath Singh, the then BJP national secretary.

After many discussions with the Joint General Secretary (Organization) Shiv Prakash Singh, BJP's National General Secretary Kailash Vijayvargiya and State Party President (Bengal) Dilip Ghosh, the party empowered six Muslim leaders (Karyakartas) at Baishnabnagar constituency to convince the Muslim voters in the six Panchayat areas that have the maximum Muslim population, which helped BJP to unite the Indians at Baisnab Nagar, irrespective of their religion and supported BJP's fight against the Bangladeshi infiltrators. In the 2016 assembly election, Baishnab Nagar was the only constituency in Malda where BJP outnumbered Congress—by 6,000 votes.

Organizational Expansion of BJP in West Bengal

After 2015, lot of attention was given to the details in

West Bengal, which became evident when Dilip Ghosh was made the State unit president after Rahul Sinha, became the National Secretary of the party. Before the assembly polls 2016, the BJP West Bengal unit thoroughly revamped its party organization to place itself as a credible opposition. Initially, the wings of the party were non-active and not very effective. Within weeks of taking over as the party president of West Bengal, a former RSS pracharak, Dilip Ghosh, cracked the whip and removed several office-bearers and district presidents. The changes were made in the backdrop of growing dissent in the rank and file over outsiders, who had joined the party in Bengal after 2014, being given important positions at the expense of old-timers. The change appears to have infused a new lease of energy with BJP Youth Wing (BJYM) hitting the streets in various parts of the state as part of the law-violation program. Actress-turned-politician Rupa Ganguly was made the chief of state BJP women's wing. In March, 2016 before the polls, BJP Bengal organized two marches or yatras. 'Nari Samman Yatra' by the BJP Mahila Morcha highlighted the lack of security for women in the state under the TMC rule. And 'Infosys to Singur' yatra was organized by the BJP Yuva Morcha. But all these efforts perhaps were not enough at that stage. The BJP's vote share dropped from 17% in the 2014 parliamentary election to just 10.2% in the 2016 assembly election. BJP Bengal realized what was wrong and started working on it. Several months went into putting a team in each of the 78,000-odd polling booths in West Bengal and to achieve that goal, BJP initiated many steps to strengthen the organization in Bengal.

One of the major roadblocks for the BJP in Bengal was the organizational feuds and disputes. Some of the units did not operate on party guidelines and thus a lot of fractions hampered the party to operate as a cohesive unit. All the senior leaders of the state were bought to complete sync-up and the disputes were resolved through many meetings, sync up discussions, and senior-level workshops. Through one-to-one coordination, the man responsible for organizational excellence in three states (Uttarakhand, Uttar Pradesh, and West Bengal), Shiv Prakash and Kailash Vijayvargiya, a stalwart in Madhya Pradesh politics having roots from ABVP focused on ground level meetings and review meetings with senior state leaders, tried to have a good clarity towards the common goal and vision of BJP in West Bengal, which started uniting the forces. Team meetings became a regular activity and helped to develop a great sense of team spirit. BJP State President, Dilip Ghosh helped to realize the central team's strategy. His experience as a Vibhag-Pracharak in RSS days also helped in emphasising the importance of grass-root connectivity and activation of strategic-level planning. The trio who have their roots from the Sangh Parivar have good sync-up as a team and have the same ideological basics, which helped them to work as a team on various issues.

Some of the major works done in the expansion of the organization in Bengal were:

Continuous Thinking Sessions: Known as 'baithaks' in party proceedings, the focus remained on continuous brainstorming over various issues. BJP West Bengal has been able to do a wonderful job in enabling every worker with some task, so that everyone is engaged with the party's vision & mission. It helped every worker to stay engaged and connected with the party's mainstream. Thus all the party workers were assigned roles and responsibilities after various rounds of thinking sessions.

Review: All the above were followed up with a monthly review and at times, it become weekly. This same process was implemented in each district. It resulted in more activities on the ground, which eventually led to greater visibility among the people of West Bengal. This attracted the masses to join BJP.

The above efforts needed a lot of focus, discipline, and more importantly fearless attitude. The political situation of Bengal was then highly intolerant for the BJP workers. But Shah's 'Silent Warrior' was unstoppable. Shiv Prakash penetrated to the deepest areas of the Naxalite movement as well that too without any protection. Shiv Prakash said in a meeting "Success mantra is to define the goal with lots of planning, homework and thinking about the steps of execution". The organizational expansion which is mainly a responsibility of Sangathan Mantri rested upon largely with Shiv Prakash and Subroto Chattopadhyay, state general secretary organization and deputy to Shiv Prakash . The organizational expansion gave a lot of jitters to on-ground TMC goons.

It was the right time to make string coordination to gain more ground in Bengal. The BJP Bengal managed to build a team of grassroot workers in every booth and this helped increase the organisation's footprint in Bengal. And it was possible under the leadership of Shiv Prakash, Kailash Vijayvargiya, Dilip Ghosh, and the other leaders of the organization. The number of mandals—the smallest organizational unit in the party—increased from 454 to about 1,162. This helped the BJP accommodate more workers as the party's office-bearers, but that was not enough. BJP realized they need more leaders who would bring votes with them This led to the formulation of a two-winged strategy.

First, the BJP made a well-planned decision to shed its

image as a party of Hindi - speaking people. This was done by giving prominence to Bengali - speaking leaders; Hindi-speaking leaders were asked to keep a low profile.

Second, BJP tapped prominent leaders of the opposition who were not happy in their parties. Former railway minister Mukul Roy of the Trinamool Congress, the one-time organizational man of West Bengal Chief Minister Mamata Banerjee, joined BJP in 2017 and helped the BJP to identify potential leaders from TMC and other parties who wanted to join hands with BJP.

Amit Shah's 'Revitalise' Mantra

As early as September 2016, Amit Shah had started a contingency plan for the 2019 elections–in case the party failed to retain the seats it won in 2014. For that, he planned to zoom in on states where the party had not made deep inroads, including southern and eastern states. A core committee meeting chaired by Shah had identified around 115 seats as the party's "New Catchment Area". In these seats, across Odisha, West Bengal, Andhra Pradesh, Telangana, Tamil Nadu, Kerala, and the Northeast, general secretaries and other office bearers were given charge.

In 2014, soon after the BJP came to power, Shah set aside the first year–2014–15–to "revitalize" the party. On 1st November 2014, six months after the BJP won a clear majority in the Lok Sabha, Shah launched his party's membership drive with the slogan 'Saath Aaye, Desh Banaye (Come together, build the nation)'. By July 2015, the membership, registered through a simple process of missed calls, rose from 3.5 crore to 11 crore. Shah then launched the 'Maha Sampark Abhiyan' or the mass contact program to familiarise new members with the organization and its ideology. He then kicked off 'Mera

Booth SabseMazboot', another campaign to take the party ideology to the booth level.

In 2017, Shah launched 'Deendayal Upadhyay Vistarak Yojana' from Naxalbari in West Bengal, setting off on a 95-day all-India tour to strategize on ways to win the 2019 Lok Sabha election, with a clear focus on 120 seats where the party had lost in the last election.

□

BJP's Mission Bengal 2019

Amit Shah's 'Mission Bengal' from Naxalbari and Launch of Vistarak Yojna

"Reached Naxalbari in West Bengal and launched Pandit Deen Dayal Upadhyay Vistarak (expansionist) Yojana, a grassroots movement to strengthen party at the booth", tweeted Amit Shah at 4.38 pm on April 25, 2017. Intending to increase BJP's footprints in West Bengal, the party president Amit Shah started the show from Naxalbari—the place where a radical-left movement started in the 1960s. "This is where the violence started. I am happy to see the Lotus bloom here," said Amit Shah on NDTV. Shah invited his cadre to take up the role of party 'vistaraks' by devoting themselves to the cause of booth level expansion. BJP took this 'Vistarak Yojana' very seriously and ensured the BJP's ideological thought and Modi government's achievements being communicated by more than 3,80,000 Vistaraks to the people.

> ***Intending to increase BJP's footprints in West Bengal, the party president Amit Shah started the show from Naxalbari—the place where a radical-left movement started in the 1960s.***

The then National General Secretary (Organisation) BJP,

Ramlal chose his deputy Shiv Prakash for this mammoth task. His role was to enable the plan of Vistaraks on the ground within a stipulated time-frame. Shiv Prakash who came from RSS as a Kshetra Pracharak, travelled extensively to all the nooks and corners of the country for the Vistarak Yojana. There were short-term Vistaraks, known as alp-kaalik-vistaraks, who left their personal and professional duties to work full time for 15 days. The next level was assembly-wise vistaraks who worked for a year or so. There were vistaraks deputed in every parliamentary seat who were working full time for more than a year and became an effective channel of communication to the central leadership. Shiv Prakash had one-on-one meeting with all of them during his visits in the states. The entire effort was monitored and followed up on a micro-level. This entire Yojana had a very significant and critical role in West Bengal.

Till then, the West Bengal BJP did not have a strong party base and always had struggled to make a mark even in the third position in any of the elections and lacked decent presence as an organization in some of the districts in terms of the booth and Mandal level. It was indeed a difficult task for the vistaraks to operate in one of the most politically violent states in the country. Shiv Prakash Ji, who himself rose to the ranks of Kshetra-pracharak starting from a tehsil-pracharak (Tehsil also known as Taluka or Taluk) with an experience of working in an adverse situation in the mountains of Uttarakhand enabled an ecosystem which helped him to find full time party workers and a cadre base in Bengal. The Sangh Parivar's ideological units extended a warm help towards BJP's Vistarak (expansionist) Yojana.

BJP's success in winning 18 constituencies in West Bengal and 8 in Odisha in 2019 Lok Sabha polls was the result of micro-level planning by party president Amit Shah. The BJP chief's emphasis on ensuring his party presence in every booth became a model strategy for other political parties.

The Vistarak yojna not only helped to win West Bengal but it created an excellent eco system of political communication in democracy. It had a wider effect in the country and henceforth enabled a deeper reach of Prime minister Narendra Modi's work to the grass root level. In total it was a benchmark for micromanagement by any standards of organizational management. DeenDayal Vistarak yojna definitely is the only example in modern Indian political history of having a country level outreach in a country like us which has diversity and vividness beyond imagination.

Strength of BJP: 2017 Ram Navami Rally at Kolkata

The turning point for Bengal politics, of course, was the Ram Navami of 2017. The 5th of April, 2017, was the day when the future of West Bengal politics was changed forever. Before that, Bengal only got a clear hint of BJP's presence at the Assembly Election results in 2016, when BJP contested in a total of 291 seats, managing to win only 3 with a vote-share of 10.16%. It was a distant third in a three-way battle between the Trinamool Congress, the Communist-Congress, and itself. BJP showed its organizational strength in 2017 Ram Navami rallies at Kolkata. After a long time RSS resurfaced the in-depth cultural nationalism on the soil of Swami Vivekananda. Then

> ***On 5th April 2017, the massive Ram Navami rallies, apart from being a great show of strength, also had a deep psychological impact on everyone. It made it clear to every single citizen in the state that the BJP was now a viable alternative.***

RSS pracharaks enabled a surge for the soul of bengal.

On 5th April 2017, the massive Ram Navami rallies, apart from being a great show of strength, also had a deep psychological impact on everyone. It made it clear to every single citizen in the state that the BJP was now a viable alternative. The Left was thrashed by Trinamool Congress in consecutive state elections; Congress was never really a credible alternative. Thus, for those who were sick and tired of Mamata's Sultanate, there remained only one viable alternative, the same one which was on a rise nationally and had a leader with great personal credibility. From that point on, the BJP never looked back.

It is important to appreciate the massive organizational strength that the BJP developed in an extremely short period, compared to Assembly Election results in 2016. Until the end of the Assembly Elections, saffron was virtually nonexistent in the state as a viable alternative. There were no college campuses or universities, where ABVP or BJYM could be perceived to be a force of strength. It was only after the Assembly Elections were over, that the BJP started working on developing its organizational infrastructure in the state massively. And it happened pretty quickly. BJP Karyakartas started becoming a lot more visible around college campuses and universities, supporters started getting a lot more vocal than they previously were, foot soldiers of the party became active on the ground and by the end of 2016, it appeared certain that the BJP was going to become a very potent force in the state.

High Tide in Bengal BJP

The BJP started building a strong mass-based foundation. And instead of having a top-heavy structure, its karyakartas reached out to people in the decentralized enterprise. Each of the 20-odd blocks in a district was treated as a Mandal of 300 booths with roughly 40,000-50,000 voters. Each Mandal was run by a committee of 12-36 members. Working under the Mandals were Shakti Pramukhs, with the specific target of increasing the party's presence in five to six booths; Booth Palaks were given the responsibility of targeting two booths, or 2,000 voters each. The party engaged Panna Pramukhs to shadow 30-50 voters in each locality, befriending them and solving their problems. Party workers were made office-bearers of organizational units to give them a sense of ownership of the mission. Though each of the districts ended up having 30–40 leaders, it was never a case of too many cooks, as each was assigned a specific job and, irrespective of rank, given to understand that they were all Shah's foot soldiers in Bengal. Within one and a half years, the party increased the number of mandals from 484 to 1162, Shakti Kendras from zero to 12,404 with more than 10,000 Shakti Pramukhs, and booth committees from zero to 58,000.

The party also appointed 300 Vistaraks for each of the 294 constituencies. These were full time workers, getting a monthly allowance of Rs 15,000, accommodation, and a bike to travel to rural areas. The job of a vistarak was to set up a camp in a constituency, oversee organizational work, and send weekly reports to the party headquarters. The party also created separate cells of teachers, advocates, musical troupes, and Matuas (Bangladeshi Dalits who had crossed over to West Bengal).

The BJP also started stitching up social alliances by joining hands with the other political outfits such as the Greater Cooch Behar People's Association (an outfit of the Rajbongshi community that influences in about half-a-dozen Lok Sabha seats of North Bengal), the Kamtapur Progressive Party of Atul Roy, a Gorkha Janmukti Morcha faction led by Bimal Gurung, and the Gorkha National Liberation Front.

This strategy successfully made a strong presence of BJP in North Bengal, which was evident in Panchayat Elections 2018 in the state where, despite suppressed election by the Trinamool, the BJP did as well in areas with a significant tribal population. It also emerged the second strongest party in the state, ahead of the Left Front and the Congress.

The Panchayat Elections of West Bengal 2018

In the year 2018, it became abundantly clear once and for all that Trinamool's primary opposition was the Bharatiya Janata Party. Panchayat Elections were around the corner and the atmosphere was electric. The 2018 Panchayat Elections saw Trinamool embracing tactics that were the hallmark of the Left regime. Extreme violence and voter intimidation became the norm. Numerous BJP Karyakartas were murdered or thrashed, even candidates were not spared. The state police were responsible of colluding with the government in suppressing the BJP in the state through threats and other means. Despite all of that, the BJP managed to improve greatly upon its 2013 Panchayat poll performance.

The Trinamool Congress won an unprecedented number of seats, 33 percent of 50000 seats uncontested as well, which was further indicative of the violent nature of Mamata's regime. While even Trinamool managed to improve upon its earlier performance, the Left and Congress were utterly decimated. Thus, it became clear once and for all, that Trinamool's primary opposition going forward would be the BJP.

In 2018 Panchayat polls, which was marred by violence, saw the BJP win 18 percent of the seats, giving it the confidence to prepare for the Lok Sabha polls. Panchayats in West Bengal are seen as powerful tools to control at the ground level. Almost 52 BJP workers were killed in the run-up to the panchayat polls. The levels of violence were so unprecedented that there was unusual evidence of candidates of BJP, Congress and Left candidates going together to file their nominations to avoid attacks by the TMC. The three parties approached the courts as civic polls are conducted under the watch of the State Election Commission and not the ECI. The three parties together blamed Mamata's TMC for the threats and violence—which ensured that the TMC won 33 percent of seats uncontested.

Technology Push: Using the New Media for 'Mission Bengal'

Call centres, GPS-fitted Raths, videos and hologram addresses, and tracking of booths and volunteers—the BJP's campaign over the yesteryears has been infused with technology. For the 2019 election, the party had 168 call centers with 12,662 karyakartas, who would contact people on the telephone or through social media. Shah has incorporated high-tech designers and consultants in his team.

A 15,000-member WhatsApp group of the party reached out to 1.5 million voters. The BJP started a social media cell, under its national IT Cell head Amit Malviya...

A 15,000-member WhatsApp group of the party reached out to 1.5 million voters. The BJP started a social media cell, under its national IT Cell head Amit Malviya, with 10,000 people to reach areas where the party was finding it hard to penetrate due to the strong presence of the TMC. About 50,000 WhatsApp groups were created, with a target of delivering messages to 30 million smartphones in the state.

Selection of the Right Candidate

From stitching up new social coalitions to choosing the right leaders for election management, Amit Shah was arguably the last word in organisational matters. In Bengal, his trusted lieutenants Shiv Prakash and other leaders along with Kailash Vijayvargiya executed exactly his style of action.

When it comes to choosing people to do the job, nothing comes in Shah's way except the candidate's ability to accomplish the mission. "There's no lobby in the BJP. If Shah is convinced that you can do the job, you are in, its about hard work on ground."

For instance in Bengal, BJP needed a bahubali like Nisith Pramanik (sidelined TMC youth leader from Cooch Behar) to take on another bahubali leader (Rabindra Nath Ghosh); the BJP Bengal did it without any hesitation. This allowed defectors from the Left and TMC to contest as BJP candidates from Barrackpoure, Jadavpur, Diamond Harbour, Bishnupur, Malda North, Malda South, and Jangipur Lok Sabha constituency.

BJP selected Debasree Chaudhuri for Raiganj, the most tightly contested seat in West Bengal. Raiganj witnessed a neck and neck four-corner fight between CPI(M), TMC, Congress, and BJP. Debasree Chaudhuri won the election with a margin of 60, 574 votes. At Darjeeling, BJP selected Raju Singh Bista, a businessman of Manipuri origin and Raju Singh won the election by 4,13,443 margin of votes. BJP's candidate Locket Chatterjee won the Hooghly constituency (with a margin of 73,362 votes), from where Mamata Banerjee started her journey to capture the left citadel.

Candidates were also selected keeping in mind the

demographic composition. BJP barely got time for campaigning in the first two phases in areas like North Bengal. So BJP Bengal fielded known faces-John Barla, a tribal labour leader from the tea gardens, from the Alipurduar seat; and Kunar Hembram, the engineer who programmed software for the Ol Chiki script, was fielded from a tribal seat in Jhargram. A former Left MLA Khagen Murmu, with a strong base in Malda district, was allowed to contest immediately after joining the party. Accusing Mamata of minority appeasement, the BJP advocated the need for a majority narrative. In Malda, a minority-dominated district, 48 percent Hindus voted for the BJP. While the BJP won in one seat-Malda(N) and lost Malda(S) only by 8,000 votes.

Save Bengal Campaign

A unique nationwide campaign–the brainchild of the Sangathan Mantri Shiv Prakash -'Save Bengal' was the nationwide civil society movement that emerged on the eve of 2019 Lok Sabha election, led by the party president Amit Shah and BJP's Bengal commander Shiv Prakash. It was a "non-political" platform for professionals and intellectuals to highlight the "misgovernance" of the Mamata Banerjee-led Trinamul Congress (TMC). 'Save Bengal' campaign played a major role in highlighting how the BJP is the "only credible alternative" to the "TMC's misrule" in the state. Under the campaign, seminars, intellectual meets, and group discussions were held by professionals, including those living outside the state, on issues concerning the state. The campaign was launched ahead of the Lok Sabha polls. Many Bengalis were miffed with the TMC and its governance and wanted to associate with the "BJP's efforts" but without joining the party, and the campaign gave them an opportunity. The BJP already had a data bank of nearly 5,000 volunteers, mostly professionals, but many homemakers, including from the state, who wanted to "associate and contribute" to the campaign. Many of these volunteers were also "social media warriors", who played a key role in the recently concluded Lok Sabha polls. The movement aimed at 'building awareness' among Bengalis living in major cities outside and of West Bengal about the 'lack of democratic space' in the state so that those people could, in turn, influence the opinion of their relatives and friends living in West Bengal. The 360-degree nationwide campaign was formally launched at the Constitution Club in New Delhi on November 24, 2018. In that event, BJP's National joint general secretary (organisation) Shiv Prakash, In-charge of party's Bengal unit, State President Dilip Ghosh, Rajya Sabha MP Swapan Dasgupta, and Dr. Syama Prasad Mookerjee Foundation Chairman Anirban Ganguly discussed on the 'Problem State' West Bengal along with former Air Marshal Amal Kumar Mukhopadhyaya and retired Major General of the Army, PK Mallick.

'Save Bengal' created an opportunity for the Bengalis across India and abroad to be united as volunteers and fight against the atrocities of Mamata Government and to remove the sense of despondency amongst people of Bengal and infuse positive energy in them. The campaign aimed to fight for the rule of law and also to create awareness about the loss of democratic space in present-day Bengal. 'Save Bengal' arranged seminars and addas (chat sessions) to reinforce the pride in Bengal's legendary heroes- Netaji Subhas Chandra Basu, Swami Vivekananda, Chaitanya Mahaprabhu, Syamaprasad Mookerjee, RabindranathTagore, Ishwar Chandra Vidyasagar, Bankim Chandra Chatterjee, Aurobindo Ghosh to name a few.

The main vision of the campaign was to increase awareness among the educated elite and influencers on the concerns it has been raising concerning West Bengal. The 'Save Bengal' campaign aimed to re-instill among resident and non-resident (Probashi) Bengalis a sense of pride in their heritage and give them a platform to voice their concerns without a sense of fear. The like-minded group of professionals, academics, lawyers, retired defence personnel, doctors, writers, homemakers wished to see Bengal regain her lost glory and once again take a position of leadership–economic, industrial, trade, and finance. Bengalis across all spectrums need to reinvent the cultural ethos, spearhead transformation, and create a positive narrative.

The main vision of the campaign was to increase awareness among the educated elite and influencers on the concerns it has been raising concerning West Bengal. The 'Save Bengal' campaign aimed to re-instill among resident and non-resident (Probashi) Bengalis a sense of pride in their heritage and give them a platform to voice their concerns without a sense of fear.

BJP introduced 'Save Bengal' chapters in different parts of the country and districts of West Bengal to hold talks and panel discussions on the 'Trouble State' West Bengal. During the campaign, people from different sections came forward and raised the issue of everyday political violence, vanishing investments, growing unemployment, organised extortion or 'Tolabaji' in educational institutions, Syndicate Raj and minority appeasement in the state, which obstructed social-economic growth.

□

BJP's Operation Bengal 2019: The X Factor and the Masterminds

According to many political analysts and pundits, 'Modi-Shah' was the X factor in the 2019 Lok Sabha election in West Bengal and none other than Mamata Banerjee could sense it very well. Both Shah and Prime Minister Narendra Modi devoted a major part of their campaign time to Bengal. They addressed 15 rallies each in the state. Both sought to take advantage of the "disenchantment" among Hindus over the growing population of Muslim migrants, a "threat" to the state's development and security. Moreover, they created many 'Invisible Factors' in the state, which silently made a huge gain for the BJP in Bengal.

Shah's six lieutenants who made Lotus Bloom in Bengal

In 2018, when Amit Shah said BJP would win 23 of 42 seats in Mamata's Bengal, many political pundits of Bengal laughed at it. But Shah and his lieutenants, Party General Secretary, Kailash Vijayvargiya and Joint General Secretary (Organization), Shiv Prakash kept chipping away before the BJP launched its final onslaught, breaking the Trinamool Congress citadel and making deep inroads.

Shiv Prakash : The Political Trainer

Shiv Prakash, a former RSS Pracharak, worked closely with Shah in the 2014 Lok Sabha polls and was promoted for his work. Under his guidance, the BJP improved its vote share in the 2016 West Bengal Assembly polls and reached double digits. His extensive work at the grassroots level helped the BJP improve its vote-share in Bengal from 4.1% in the 2011 Assembly election to nearly 11% in 2016. Subsequently, the party improved its performance in the Panchayat elections and increased its vote-share from 17% in the 2014 general election to 40% in 2019 Lok Sabha Election in West Bengal.

> ***A trained RSS Pracharak, Shiv Prakash, the BJP's Sah-Sangathan Maha Mantri, played a significant role in bringing party workers together as a cohesive team in Bengal. After getting responsibility from party president for Bengal, he was involved in the "intricate planning" of campaigning, imparted "political training" to workers, and helped them understand the pulse of the electorate of Bengal.***

A trained RSS Pracharak, Shiv Prakash, the BJP's Sah-Sangathan Maha Mantri, played a significant role in bringing party workers together as a cohesive team in Bengal. After getting responsibility from party president for Bengal, he was involved in the "intricate planning" of campaigning, imparted "political training" to workers, and helped them understand the pulse of the electorate of Bengal. A patient listener, Shiv Prakash, who is well-regarded in the Sangh Parivar for his grassroots work, is considered to have played a key role in western Uttar Pradesh in the 2014 Lok Sabha elections. He started his journey as the tehsil pracharak of Hasanpur (the then Moradabad district of Western UP) in 1986 Shiv Prakash was RSS pracharak in Meerut, Almora, and Dehradun before being promoted as prantpracharak of Uttarakhand (2000-09) and kshetrapracharak of Pashchim Kshetra (Uttarakhand and western UP) in 2014. On 7th July 2014, the RSS loaned him to the BJP. Since then, as the BJP's Sangathan Mantri, he is in charge of organisational matters of West Bengal, Uttar Pradesh, and Uttarakhand BJP unit.

Shiv Prakash worked behind the scenes in working out social combinations, ironing out organisational glitches, and keeping the BJP's election machine running efficiently in the three states. He played a key role in West Bengal by appointing teams from booth level to district level. Given special responsibilities to look into the organisational matters in West Bengal, he worked to strengthen the party's grass root presence and also helped to remove the BJP's organisational shortcomings in Bengal and gave leadership in setting up confident election machinery, by putting in place teams to ensure strong booth-level organisations.

The party president Amit Shah sent Vijayvargiya and Shiv Prakash Singh to oversee party efforts in the state in 2015. Vijayvargiya is known for his two special traits. Most of the time, he prefers to introduce bhajans to convey messages to party workers, instead of making lengthy speeches.

Shiv Prakash and Vijayvargiya: A Perfect Combination

BJP started working in Bengal ever since it was swept to power in 2014. The party president Amit Shah sent Vijayvargiya and Shiv Prakash to oversee party efforts in the state in 2015.

Vijayvargiya is known for his two special traits. Most of the time, he prefers to introduce bhajans to convey messages to party workers, instead of making lengthy speeches. Secondly, he can instil the "killer instinct" in party workers.

Shiv Prakash and Kailash Vijayvargiya, both the leaders worked on social combinations, resolved internal issues within the organisation and scouted for the right people to work on the ground. The growth was amazing. From 452 mandal committees in 2015, it went up to 1,280. In four years, it was ready with 12,407 Shakti Kendras, 10,266 Shakti Kendra pramukhs, and 58,084 committees. The state was divided into five segments for managing the Lok Sabha constituencies.

The party won 18 percent votes in the Panchayat elections in 2018, despite the TMC's uncontested win in 33 percent of the panchayats. This gave new momentum to the party and became the pivot for a concerted campaign associating TMC with violence.

The 'Vijayvargiya and Prakash' combination played a key role from behind the scenes in capturing Mukul Roy from the Trinamool and provided him the much-needed backing to ensure the defection of several leaders from the ruling party in the state, several of whom were made candidates in the 2019 Lok Sabha elections.

Arvind Menon: The Disrupter

On October 3, 2018, Amit Shah appointed national executive member Arvind Menon as its Bengal co-minder. Menon had played a key role in the 2017 Gujarat assembly election. BJP's national executive member and Bengali-speaking RSS pracharak Arvind Menon also played a significant role in BJP's 'Mission Bengal', after he was appointed in January 2019 as co-incharge and observer for the Lok Sabha elections in the state, reporting directly to the BJP President Amit Shah. Menon was assisted by Mukul Roy, who was made the election in-charge. Menon first focused on North Bengal, and blended the BJP with the Sangh all along Darjeeling to Malda. The success they aimed at could be seen, for example, in Raiganj in North Bengal, where 47 per cent of the voters are Hindus and 53 per cent Muslims. Hindus were up in arms in September 2018, over the killing of two ABVP members in police firing. There was violence again, and two more deaths, when the state government appointed Urdu teachers to the posts left vacant by science teachers at a high school. Local people buried, not cremated, the two dead bodies so that they could be exhumed for re-investigation, if the BJP came to power.

Suresh Pujari: A Fearless Fighter

Odisha BJP leader, one of the party's National Secretaries Suresh Pujari was sent to West Bengal as the co-in-charge in 2018. 'Prakash-Vijayvargiya' duo put Suresh Pujari as the in-charge of the South Western districts of Bengal.

Pujari's political activism started in his student days in Odisha. He became famous after leading an agitation demanding fee waiver for poor college students. The agitation turned violent and ultimately the state government had to budge. Pujari joined the BJP in 1997 and became president of the Odisha state unit of the party in 2006.

Along with Odisha, he is also in charge of West Bengal's Western belt including Purulia, Bankura, and Midnapore. The BJP almost smashed the ruling TMC in the West and South-West of West Bengal in the Lok Sabha Election 2019.

Dilip Ghosh – An Unstoppable Warrior

Ghosh, who worked as the in-charge of RSS in Andaman

and Nicobar Islands, was chosen as the party's Bengal unit President in 2015. In 2016, he fought the state Assembly elections from Kharagpur Sadar and defeated veteran Congress leader Gyan Singh Sohanpal. He tasted yet another success in 2019, when he won the difficult Midnapore Lok Sabha seat, defeating veteran politician Manas Bhunia of the Trinamool Congress. Since becoming the state chief, Ghosh played a pivotal role in strengthening the party infrastructure. Known for his fiery speeches, Ghosh is extremely popular among the party activists for his straight as an arrow attitude. His personality and attitude gave strength to the BJP activists across the state to counter Trinamool's aggressiveness.

Mukul Roy–A Deadly Defector

Mukul Roy helped spread the BJP's reach to the grassroot level of North 24 Parganas and Nadia, besides inducing several Trinamool MPs and MLAs to the BJP. Roy, well known for his organisational skills and close connection with the Trinamool's grassroots level leaders, was given the responsibility of the chief election strategist by the BJP in Bengal. Arjun Singh, the TMC MLA from Barrackpore, Cooch Behar TMC youth leader Nisith Pramanik, Bolpur TMC MP Anupam Hazra, and Bishnupur TMC MP Soumitra Khan -- all came to the saffron camp at Roy's behest and were given tickets for the Lok Sabha polls. Arjun Singh, Soumitra Khan, and Nisith Pramanik won from their respective constituencies.

Mukul Roy is one of those who helped re-engineer Bengal's voting pattern twice in recent history–first in 2011, when the TMC wiped out the Communist Party of India (Marxist)'s 34-year-long rule in the state and then in 2019, when the BJP – in Bengal – captured almost half the electorate by winning 18 out of the 42 Parliament seats in the state. He was one of the vital factors under the guidance of 'Prakash–Vijayvargiya' duo. In his new avatar as a BJP leader in Bengal, Mukul Roy used his old strategies to induct TMC deserters to strengthen the base of the BJP, but this time he only did that as a team member, after careful consultation with Sangathan Mantri Shiv Prakash and State Observer Kailash Vijayvargiya, and of course, some of the TMC deserters like Arjun Singh have proved to be useful.

The 'Invisible' strength of BJP in Bengal

The rise of BJP in Bengal began soon after the 2014 Lok Sabha elections. The BJP deployed RSS stalwarts Kailash Vijayvargiya and Shiv Prakash as state in-charges. BJP's Sangathan Mantri Singh's biggest challenge was to bring a 'parivartan' (change) in Bengal, because it became a concern as far as national security (due to illegal immigrants) is a concern. In 2015, he was given the responsibility of Bengal and since then, his primary job was to ensure better coordination among party cadres and win the confidence of Bengali people Sangh also strength its reach via shakhas and enabled a greater presence of its Vichar Parivar. This was a very tough work considering the violence Swayam-Sevak have to face everyday in West Bengal. Kshetra Pracharak Pradip Joshi who still travels by public transportation enabled a very deep reach of Shakhas which is still expanding. From 2014–2019, the RSS started 3,000 branches in the state and many schools in far-flung villages and tribal areas. Numerous shakhas with school and college students as members also came up.

The number of BJP mandals—the smallest unit of the party—increased from 452 to 1,280 in three years, expanding the number of stakeholders within the party set-up. The state was divided into five zones—Uttar Banga, Navadeep, Rar Banga, Hooghly Midnapur, and Kolkata—with each of them comprising about eight Lok Sabha seats. A well thought out strategy, well-oiled party machinery, and months of rigorous preparation stood the BJP in good stead in the election. Amit Shah personally monitored improvement on each of these fronts. A well-oiled Election Management team operated by the state secretary Deepanjan Guha and Sutanu Roy in party head office also enabled to implement the strategy on ground.

RSS-BJP enabled turning North Bengal Saffron

The RSS has been present in North Bengal for the last two decades, but expansion in the North of Bengal had not happened before. In 2015, Adwaitacharan Dutta was replaced as kshetra pracharak (in-charge North Bengal, South Bengal, Odisha, Sikkim, and Andaman) by Pradip Joshi (formerly pranta pracharak of Arunachal Pradesh). After that-trends of the 2016 Assembly polls, the by-elections, Civic polls, and the 2019 Lok Sabha election held since, however, reveal the Sangh Parivar's growing influence in refugee colonies of North Bengal who migrated from Bangladesh over the past few decades. In 2016, BJP surprisingly won two assembly seats in North Bengal, Madarihat and Baishnabnagar constituency and in the meantime, RSS made a strong penetration in Naxalbari area of North Bengal, a former stronghold of radical left movement, where Amit Shah started his 'Mission Bengal' rally in 2017. Incidentally, Prime Minister Narendra Modi's 2019 poll campaign on Mamata Banerjee's turf didn't start from Kolkata, but North Bengal.

RSS Swayamsevaks made their strong presence felt in North Bengal

In 2018–19, The total number of RSS shakhas in North Bengal had grown to approximately 500, an almost three-fold increase since 2010, located in Cooch Behar and Alipurduar, along with Darjeeling, Jalpaiguri, and Raiganj, which proved a key factor because of the nature of the seats and its electorate. Of the five seats, three are reserved either for tribals (Alipurduar) or Dalits (Cooch Behar, Jalpaiguri), while all are dominated by tea estate workers.

The RSS's plan for expansion in North Bengal had largely been two-fold, to concentrate on tea workers' unions and the rights of Adivasis through the Bhartiya Mazdoor Sangh (BMS), or through an expansive network of schools and grassroot organisations that have worked extensively with the rural poor. In Alipurduar's Lok Sabha constituency, for instance, the swayamsevaks (RSS workers) work actively with tribals. They have improved their network in other areas of the region too, including Siliguri. The RSS-affiliated Vanvasi Kalyan Ashram runs a school in Siliguri for the children of tea garden workers, who are mostly tribals. With the growth in the shakhas, the number of swayamsevaks has also increased to more than 20,000 across North Bengal, mainly in pockets in Siliguri, Jalpaiguri, Cooch Behar, and Alipurduar.

In 2019 election, BJP managed 47.98%, 54.40% and 50.65% vote shares at Cooch Behar, Alipurduar and Jalpaiguri constituency respectively. At Raiganj and Balurghat constituency, BJP acquired 40.06% and 45.02% vote shares. The BJP gained well in Darjeeling because of the support of the Gorkha Janmukti Morcha Worker Union, that had been working in the tea estates. BJP's candidate, Raju Bista from Darjeeling constituency managed 59.19% vote share in the 2019 general election West Bengal.

An admirable growth of RSS-BJP was not unknown to Mamata Banerjee, 'once close friend' of RSS-BJP, who tried to create a deep dent against BJP in North Bengal. "Babus of

Delhi set fire in the hills and we defused it. You (Modi) had not come to Darjeeling during the days of unrest. Where were the BJP leaders when there were disturbances in the hills?" she said at a rally at Churabhandar in Jalpaiguri district, hours after Modi spoke at an election meeting there in 2019. Later at Falakata in Alipurduar district, Banerjee said BJP leaders "are seasonal birds who come here only during elections and run away after polls," News18 reported. But all her efforts failed when out of the total eight seats in North Bengal, BJP won seven, barring Malda South. BJP not only retained Darjeeling but won in tribal-dominated Alipurduar and also wrested Jalpaiguri, Cooch Behar, and Balurghat from the TMC, Maldaha Uttar from Congress and Raiganj from the CPM.

Since her first election meeting in North Bengal, Mamata Bannerjee had been critical of BJP-ruled Assam on the NRC issue and the Citizenship Amendment Bill. But according to political observers, in some parts of North Bengal like Cooch Behar, Alipurduar and Jalpaiguri, Mamata Banerjee's NRC pitch went against her party.

Since her first election meeting in North Bengal, Mamata Bannerjee had been critical of BJP-ruled Assam on the NRC issue and the Citizenship Amendment Bill. But according to political observers, in some parts of North Bengal like Cooch Behar, Alipurduar and Jalpaiguri, Mamata Banerjee's NRC pitch went against her party. This is because a considerable section of people, whose family members and relatives live in Assam, were aggrieved with the state government. This happened because those people were worried as names of their family members and relatives did not figure in the NRC, reportedly because of delay on the part of the Bengal government in finishing verification of their documents, which were sent from Assam. According to a report of 'The Telegraph'-The rise in the BJP's support—right from the tea belt of the Dooars to the hills and the remote areas of Malda, and the North and South Dinajpur—is because of several other local reasons, said Trinamul insiders "The minimum tea wage is yet to be fixed by the state and this is one issue the BJP has highlighted during its campaign. Also, the steady penetration of the RSS in tribal areas and remote villages is yet another reason, that has helped the BJP gain support," said a senior Trinamul leader in Jalpaiguri.

In 2014, the BJP had won only Darjeeling, just as it had in 2009. Its vote share in North Bengal was around 22 percent. In 2019, the share jumped to 46 percent. After the 2019 election results were announced, it seems the life-size statue of Bharat Mata is smiling at Madhab Bhawan, RSS headquarter of North Bengal at Hakim Para, Siliguri. Though RSS always claimed their organization does not indulge in any political activity, many BJP leaders in Malda, Jalpaiguri, Siliguri and Cooch Behar agree that it is the RSS' work on the ground that helped the party increase its footprint in West Bengal, especially in North Bengal.

In other parts of West Bengal RSS played a key role, Kshetra pracharak Pradip Joshi and then Prant Pracharak Bidyut Mukherjee with their both team work ensured a saffron upsurge.

Team effort of all

The victory in Lok Sabha elections was the work of lakhe of BJP workers and the strength of its organisation (Sanghthan). It can only be imagined that how tough it was when young workers had to fight against regime of political eco-system which has been in place for forty years. This has been a superior effort of organisational strength. For example young team which worked under the guidance of the state general secretary (organisation-Bhartiya Janta Party) Subrato Chattopadhyay and young joint general secretary Kishor Barman worked with every district teams and extended there reach to the last mile in West Bengal. During the elections very senior organisational secretaries & Pracharaks like Amitava Chakravorty (Odhisha) and Chandrashekhar (Rajasthan). Who came to West Bengal just after their respective elections got over, to oversee party's election work. For instance Kishore Barman's role was to be the eyes and ears for organization in North Bengal, Amitava Chakravorty's vast experience in his ABVP days (in West Bengal) proved to be very critical and his strategic inputs became very critical for finalizing course of action, Chandrashekar enabled a vast reach out to the Marwari community in Kolkata and 24 Paraganas This proves the importance of West Bengal as an ideological powerhouse for all BJP worker and Vichar Pariwar volunteers. Amitava Chakravarty's insight during a meeting seemed to be the mantra for BJP in upcoming preparations, which was " welcome the new members as one of our own family and giving much deserving respect to those who have been fighting the ideological battle since a very long time" . This brilliant effort proved to be an excellent success for BJP.

From Marx to Modi : The left moves right

The Left Font's vote share in West Bengal has come down from 43% in 2009 Lok Sabha elections to 29.93% in 2014 to 7.46% in 2019 and at the same time, the BJP's share went up from 6.14% in 2009 to 17% in 2014 to 40% in 2019-almost close to Trinamool Congress' 43%, clearly indicates that the RSS-BJP is growing in Bengal as the Left-TMC both are losing trust of those people who voted many times for the Left and were also confused by the policy of Muslim appeasement of Mamata Banerjee. If this is a valid reason, then In urban areas, middle class and upper-middle-class Hindu voters silently supported BJP because religion is always an important issue in Bengal. Also, people did not like the way opposition leaders used unparliamentary language against Narendra Modi and called him a thief. Another thought on transferring left votes to BJP, came from the CPI(M) officially as Sitaram Yechury said, "No party CPI(M) member would have voted (for the BJP). But the Left vote support base, the victims of intense terror and repression of eight years of the Trinamool rule have done so." However, the Left started losing its support base much before 2019. BJP's vote share could increase by a transfer of votes from the Left, as was established in the 2016 Cooch Behar Lok Sabha by-poll, where a loss of 27 percent vote share from the Forward Bloc and its direct transfer to the BJP helped it move to the second position from fourth. Cooch Behar became a successful example of the consolidation of all anti-TMC votes in favour of the BJP.

In the 2019 Lok Sabha election, the BJP not only achieved a good result in West Bengal, but almost conquered it. The Trinamool managed to maintain its south Bengal bastion while the BJP made big inroads into the northern and western parts of the state. Lokniti's post-poll survey shows that about two-fifths of the traditional Left voters shifted to the BJP and about one third to the Trinamool Congress. Similarly, 32% of old Congress voters moved to the BJP and 29% moved to the Trinamool.

Old Left and Congress supporters moved towards BJP and TMC

Community	Voted BJP in 2019	Voted TMC in 2019	Voted Left in 2019	Voted Cong in 2019
Traditional Left Voters	39	31	30	-
Traditional Cong Voters	32	20	4	32

Source: Lokniti-CSDS Survey

The state, which in many ways is the birthplace of Hindutva and from where its founder Syama Prasad Mookerjee represented in the Parliament, had undoubtedly chosen the BJP in 2019 Lok Sabha election as the prime opposition to the Trinamool Congress. It took almost 40 years since its formation in 1980 for the Bharatiya Janata Party (BJP) to truly reach West Bengal with 18 Lok Sabha seats. For nearly 40 years, the state remained isolated from national politics. The local narrative was ruled by Leftist ideologies, which survived the politics of confrontation with the Centre. Trinamool Congress (TMC), which was also a product of this trend, is now being highly challenged by the saffron power. It's a strongly polarised new Bengal against Mamata Banerjee's misgovernance and which is not afraid to change its past loyalty, and BJP is not a political untouchable anymore in Bengal, which means the State is now, not the only ground of regional parties. At the same time, no one can probably take it for granted. The Bengal- the birthplace of Hindutva is now seeking not only a change of Government but looking for a better alternative to build a 'Sonar Bangla'- to regain its lost glory of culture and economic glory and to take an active part in Narendra Modi's 'New India'.

Bengal was waiting for a Hindu Aura of Authority

History may remember the 23rd of May, 2019 as the day when the future of Bengal Politics changed forever. However, it was on the 5th of April, 2017, on the auspicious day of Ram Navami, that the seeds of it were sown.

While great credit must go to Prime Minister Narendra Modi, Amit Shah, Shah's 'silent warrior' Shiv Prakash, Kailash Vijayvargiya, Dilip Ghosh and the respective leaders of the state unit for BJP's stellar victory in Bengal, the victory also overwhelmingly belongs to the cadres on the ground, who sacrificed their lives and risked physical violence, but ensured BJP's victory at great personal cost. It's important to understand that the BJP could never have gained ground in Bengal, if they did not speak of issues that hold great significance for Hindus of Syama Prasad's Bengal and the misgovernance of Mamata Banerjee. Illegal immigration, minority appeasement, communal violence, all these issues are of significant importance to the Bengal electorate. Unfortunately, however, there's only one party on the horizon which voices these concerns and promises to address them. Therefore, it is important to remember that valid concerns of the Bengal electorate were not addressed by any other party and the BJP rose to prominence in the state, riding on the promise to address them. The era of Religious Polarization in West Bengal (though it's not a new trend in Bengal), is further indicated by the utter collapse of the Left. It is a fact that Hindu voters of the Left crossed over to the BJP in the 2019 Lok Sabha elections and this crossover has largely been motivated by concerns that revolve around their Hindu identity. And not just Hindu upper castes, but also Other Backward Classes, Scheduled Castes, and Scheduled Tribes voted for the BJP in large proportions.

Hindu communities consolidated behind BJP, Muslims behind TMC

Community	Voted BJP 2014	Voted BJP 2019	Voted TMC 2014	Voted TMC 2019	Voted lEFT 2014	Voted LEFT 2019	Voted CONG 2014	Voted CONG 2019
Hindus	21	57	40	32	29	6	6	3
Muslims	2	4	40	70	31	10	24	12
Upper caste	24	57	38	31	27	9	5	3
OBC	21	65	43	28	26	4	4	2
Dalits	20	61	40	27	29	6	8	4
Adivasis	11	58	40	28	41	12	5	2

Source: Lokniti-CSDS Survey

Many Pundits and leaders severely underestimated the extent to which Bengal is fertile for the politics of Hindutva, though it is the land of Nationalism, the land of Swami Vivekananda and Bankim Chandra Chatterjee, the land of political 'Hindutva' of Chandranath Basu and the land of 'Bengali Hindu Homeland Movement' of Syama Prasad Mookerjee. Naturally, Hindutva could be kept away from Bengal for long but not forever. After Tripura, another state dominated by Bengalis, voted in a BJP government, it was only a matter of time before West Bengal started showing a similar trend. Hindutva only needed a face with great personal credibility and an

Hindutva only needed a face with great personal credibility and an aura of authority around him to succeed in Bengal and when Narendra Modi became its face, it was only a matter of time because Bengal politics, at the end of the day, has always been dominated by personalities and their credibility, like Syama Prasad Mookerjee.

aura of authority around him to succeed in Bengal and when Narendra Modi became its face, it was only a matter of time because Bengal politics, at the end of the day, has always been dominated by personalities and their credibility, like Syama Prasad Mookerjee.

In 2019, for the first time in its history, the Bharatiya Janata Party made a huge entry into West Bengal. The state was so much important for the BJP that Prime Minister Narendra Modi gave the second-highest number of rallies and speeches, the highest being in Uttar Pradesh. In his public meetings in West Bengal, Narendra Modi spoke at length about the developmental achievements of the National Democratic Alliance government at the Centre and termed Mamata Banerjee as the "speed breaker" in Bengal's development. He also stressed the need to restore democracy in Bengal. Unable to counter Narendra Modi politically, Mamata Banerjee resorted to personal attacks. This perhaps resulted in more voters moving towards the BJP. Narendra Modi 's strategy was successful in influencing the electorate in general and the younger voters in particular.

Ahead of the 2021 West Bengal State election, the BJP is the political party that is on the rise and Trinamool appears to be on its way down in West Bengal. Whether Mamata Banerjee will be able to stem the BJP's growth in her home turf remains to be seen. She has failed spectacularly. With her unabashed minority appeasement, it is a fact that she has alienated large sections of the Hindu community and this disgruntled section of the Hindu community, which grows in strength every day, is responsible for the BJP's rise in the state.

□

Epilogue

The year 2020 will be remembered as the year which all of us would have wished that it never existed. That was the year where human resilience was tested; it was a year where the world came to a halt. Everything came to a standstill with a pause and it is one of the most testing times in human history where the Covid virus has brought destruction to countless lives and families. It has given some sorrows which are irreversible.

In these tough times, the entire world came together. India led from the front as the world's capital of the remedy and resilience. Entire world followed up in the footsteps and has accolades of India's capability for making as well as giving Covid vaccines to the world as per the need. When the entire country was holding hand-in-hand and trying to fight one of the toughest battles, West Bengal government's confusing data on Covid death and affected persons made the national news. West Bengal government's fragile healthcare system was clearly exposed when videos of dead bodies on the streets came into surface. According to media reports, people diagnosed with Corona virus didn't even manage beds in Government hospitals without political influence. The TMC Government found itself in a total mess with its poor management to tackle the pandemic. Ironically, almost 121 years ago the plague pandemic in Bengal was successfully managed by a Hindu monk—Swami Vivekananda, vividly described in 'Plague Manifesto'.

Amphan

It was very unfortunate for the people of West Bengal to have faced two natural calamities at the same time. Firstly Covid pandemic was made worse by the TMC government's severe misrule, then Super Cyclonic Storm Amphan hit Coastal areas in West Bengal in East Midnapore, North 24 Parganas, South 24 Parganas, Kolkata, Hooghly, and Howrah. The destruction caused by Amphan in West Bengal was devastating and it completed exposed the shoddy work and poor planning of the West Bengal government. Kolkata, once the capital of the country was out of electricity supply, basic sanitation, water and food. The rural parts of the state were even worse where people had to starve for many days. We saw videos of police beating women for asking for honest distribution of relief work. TMC minister openly said that there was no planning even after advance warning of Amphan's destruction.

Residents of Kanchantala near the port area had to sit on roads demanding restoration of electricity in their areas; even after six days there was no sign of relief for them. Calcutta High Court had to order CAG (Comptroller and Auditor General) to audit the relief work. TMC's Gram Panchayat head was accused of siphoning Cyclone compensation. He submitted a list of 166 members for Amphan relief; out of 166 he put his mobile number against 100 names. He added his wife's name for relief compensation. Imagining the magnanimity of such cases across the state is impossible!

The widespread protest took place blocking roads; posters were put up against TMC leaders to oppose large scale corruption by TMC leaders. North 24 Pargana, South 24 Pargana, Howrah, Kolkata saw many such demonstrations. There are some serious allegations against the current TMC government leaders for such corruption.

Political Violence

One can imagine the watershed effect at the party workers and the administration when the Chief Minister of the state said in a public meeting "will send some people to disturb BJP, CPM meetings". This statement defines the belief of TMC in democratic values, free or fair administration.

On 10th December 2020, the entire country witnessed the state of law and order. Bharatiya Janata Party's National President J.P. Nadda's convoy moving towards Diamond Harbor was attacked in broad daylight in front of thousands of people who came to greet him. The video of stones being thrown at the cars of J.P. Nadda, Shiv Prakash, Kailaish Vijaywargiya went viral on social media and the entire country saw a glimpse of the kind of political violence which exists in West Bengal. Visuals of bricks crashing in cars scared those who saw the video and depicted that it was a planned attack. Even after Dilip Ghosh's warning of such kind of attacks against the BJP workers, the administration did not provide adequate security to the president of a national party.

One of the brick hit Shiv Prakash's associate Saurabh's head who was sitting in the car with him. Kailash Vijayvargiya's associate Prashant was hit on his chest and security personnel were also injured. The pictures of those visuals went viral on social media. This attack was meant to hit the morale of BJP workers but on the contrary it has pumped up the fighting spirit and the BJP cadre is more determined than ever to form government in West Bengal.

West Bengal will be experiencing one of the most crucial periods in its post-independence history. No state elections have been in so much focus in recent history. The upcoming 'Dharma Yuddha' as many say in West Bengal is going to be the 'Election of Identity'. The identity is associated with Bankim Chandra, Swami Vivekananda, Shri Aurobindo, Rabindranath Tagore, Netaji Subhas Chandra Bose, and many others versus the identity of corruption, brain drain, women safety, de-industrialisation, and cultural de transformation, which is a result of long term political governments under the Communists and now TMC.

It is evident and quite visible now that history will be created in May 2021. This is going to be after a long time when the Central government and West Bengal government can work hand-in-hand towards the wellness of its people. They will have the same goal of serving the land of Nationalist freedom fighters. The streets are full of BJP flags and workers are flocking into the BJP office to join the party. This incoming is from across parties Communist–Party, Congress, or TMC. If you speak to someone on the street and ask who is winning, the answer is '*BJP Asche*' means BJP is coming. The silent voter of BJP have become vocal because every person standing next to him or she is 'Joy Shree Ram'.

This sea change which is happening in West Bengal is evident and will be due to the workers and leaders of the Bharatiya Janata Party. it shall be the outcome of Prime Minister Modi's iconinc leadership and Home Minister Amit Shah's hard work during his days as National President of BJP. Hard work of Shiv Prakash during last 6 years who bought entire flock together and started seeding the winds of change. The ever-persistent sacrifice of the RSS cadre has been phenomenal and their belief in bringing true change in the land of Swami Vivekananda is about to come true. The relentless work of Kailash Vijaywargiya, Arvind Menon, Dilip Ghosh, Amitav Chakraborty, Kishore Burman, and thousands of BJP workers has enabled the positive change towards BJP. The battle of Bengal is not yet over but with great confidence, it can be said that 'The Rise of the Right' is imminent.

□□□